Understanding Television Production

Frank Iezzi has been involved in all phases of educational and commercial broadcasting, from writing and directing to producing and performing. He established the Communications Department at Hofstra University, where he has taught television and radio since 1958.

Understanding Television Production

Frank Iezzi

Prentice-Hall, Inc.,
Englewood Cliffs, New Jersey 07632

Library of Congress Cataloging in Publication Data

Iezzi, Frank.
    Understanding television production.

    Bibliography: p.
    Includes index.
    1. Television—Production and direction. I. Title.
PN1992.75.I37 1984   791.45′0232   83-13908
ISBN 0-13-937078-1
ISBN 0-13-937060-9 (A Reward book : pbk.)

© 1984 by Prentice-Hall, Inc., Englewood Cliffs, New Jersey 07632.
All rights reserved. No part of this book may be reproduced in any form
or by any means without permission in writing from the publisher.
Printed in the United States of America.

1 2 3 4 5 6 7 8 9 10

ISBN 0-13-937078-1

ISBN 0-13-937060-9 {PBK.}

Editorial/production supervision by Peter Jordan
Manufacturing buyer: Pat Mahoney
Cover design © 1984 by Jeannette Jacobs

This book is available at a special discount when ordered in
bulk quantities. Contact Prentice-Hall, Inc., General
Publishing Division, Special Sales, Englewood Cliffs, N.J. 07632.

Prentice-Hall International, Inc., *London*
Prentice-Hall of Australia Pty. Limited, *Sydney*
Prentice-Hall Canada Inc., *Toronto*
Prentice-Hall of India Private Limited, *New Delhi*
Prentice-Hall of Japan, Inc., *Tokyo*
Prentice-Hall of Southeast Asia Pte. Ltd., *Singapore*
Whitehall Books Limited, *Wellington, New Zealand*
Editora Prentice-Hall do Brasil Ltda., *Rio de Janeiro*

*To the memory of my mother,
Angiolina Roseto Iezzi, in appreciation of all she did,
gave, and was, and to the memory of my
dear friend Hans Vangkilde, Danish broadcaster,
for his contributions to his
friends, his family, his nation, and his
profession.*

CONTENTS

PREFACE xiii

1
THE AUDIO PERSON 1
STUDIO ACTIVITIES
Microphone Selection
Mounting and Placement
Cables and Connections
Microphone Plugs
CONTROL ROOM ACTIVITIES
Audio Console
Audio Turntable
Audiotape Recorder
Audiotape Cartridge Machine

2
THE LIGHTING PERSON 33
TECHNICAL ASPECTS OF LIGHTING
AESTHETIC CONSIDERATIONS
STUDIO LIGHTS
Light Sources: Bulbs
Studio Lights: Housings
Lighting Supports

LIGHTING INSTRUMENT PANEL
Contrast Ratio of Lighting
LIGHTING CONTROL
At the Instrument
At the Lighting Board
At the Camera

3

THE FLOOR PERSON 53
As Director's Surrogate
As Studio Troubleshooter
As Contact with the Talent
FLOOR PERSON AND GRAPHICS
Guiding Principles in Graphic Design
Graphics Production
Displaying and Handling Graphics

4

THE CAMERA PERSON 73
CAMERA SHOTS
Field of View
Portion of Subject Shown
Number of Persons Shown
Camera Angle
PICTORIAL COMPOSITION
Framing
Head Room
Impression of Depth
TV CAMERA CHAIN
Camera Base
Camera Mounting Head
Camera Head

5

THE SWITCHER 105
REALITY SWITCHES
SPECIAL EFFECTS SWITCHES
The Fade
The Dissolve
The Super
MORE ADVANCED SWITCHES
The Program Bus
The Preview Bus

ELECTRONIC SPECIAL EFFECTS
The Key
The Matte
The Chroma-Key
The Wipe
The Corner Insert
Split Screen

6

THE DIRECTOR 119
FUNCTIONS OF THE DIRECTOR
Prior to On-the-Air
On-the-Air
POSTPRODUCTION: THE VIDEOTAPE RECORDER
VTR Controls
Videotape Editing Methods

GLOSSARY 141

BIBLIOGRAPHY 153

INDEX 155

PREFACE

Walking into a TV control room for the first time is a little like walking into the engine room of a submarine for the first time: earnest-looking people, their faces lit by bluish flickering light, stare, seemingly transfixed, at electronic screens; in hushed tones, they issue commands into gooseneck microphones; their hands are bathed in cones of light as they manipulate knobs, levers, switches, lighted plastic buttons, and plastic reels. Walking into a TV studio is only slightly less perplexing. Half of the room is filled with lights—some shaped like half-melons, others tubular in shape and framed by black metal petals—all hanging from the ceiling and focused on a person who seems engaged in deep, intimate conversation with one of the metal boxes being wheeled about. The other half of the room is in semidarkness with people stealthily moving about; like so many Peeping Toms in the shadows, they watch the person under the lights but are not seen by him or her. The floor is covered with black spaghetti. There is much hand gesturing, as alien as the signing used by the deaf.

Who are these people? What are they doing? And what are they doing it with? These are the questions to which this book is addressed. The audience to which the book is addressed is the newcomer to TV production, whether that person is someone taking a course in TV at an academic institution, someone interested in participating in his or her company's closed-circuit TV training center, someone thinking about participating in productions at a local cable station or at one of the 4000 emerging low-power local TV stations, or indeed, someone curious about what goes on in a TV studio/control room.

Why another book on TV production?

xiii

First, because the information in this field is highly perishable. It ages quickly. Between the time the writer has typed the last word of the manuscript and the reader sees the first word of the printed text, much of the material is already out of date. At this writing, Sony is introducing a compact, laser-based, digital audio disc and player that could eventually make all current record players obsolete. Sony soon will mass-market an electronic still camera that will electronically record snapshots on magnetic discs instead of film, enabling customers to show them immediately—without processing—on their home TV sets. A number of companies are bringing out flat-screen TV sets employing crystal-display technology. For example, Seiko is introducing a TV wristwatch, operated by two small batteries, that can receive VHF and UHF channels, that features a flat, liquid display screen and a stereo headset for sound. Sony and Matsushita are setting aside their competing systems and are developing a joint format for a new miniature video camera/recorder, an all-in-one machine about the size of an 8mm movie camera using a videocassette about the size of a cigarette pack. Even while this manuscript was being typed, three television equipment advances were announced—any of which may—or may not—make obsolete in the 1980s every piece of TV equipment in use today. One of these developments, High Definition Television (HDTV), promises that within this decade, homes, schools, and businesses may be capable of receiving wall-sized, clearly focused, high definition color TV pictures and stereophonic sound as refined as those now shown in commercial 35mm movie theaters.

How will this be possible? Sony has just demonstrated a 1125-line TV picture with more than twice the 525-line picture definition the U.S. currently uses and a screen width-to-height ratio of 5 to 3, as opposed to the 4 to 3 ratio in use today, thereby achieving in quality and shape a truly cinematic effect. The second of these developments is Direct Broadcast Satellite (DBS), a system with which TV programs beamed to satellites would rain down across the entire country to any house or business with an antenna the size of a pizza plate that can be mounted on a roof or hung out a window. Conceivably, local, network, and cable stations could become obsolete, serving only as middlemen between the program material and the program consumer. The third of these advances, designed by three engineering professors, provides three-dimensional, stereoscopic TV pictures. In television technology, the only constant is change.

The second rationale for this book is that there simply is room—and need—for a book to serve as an introduction, a sort of primer, to TV production. My research indicates that many of the texts offer more technical data than the beginning student of TV needs—or wants. Many of the texts are geared to large professional broadcast operations with state-of-the-art equipment and facilities. This book attempts to relate to the small/medium nonbroadcast TV installation which probably has a modest budget, modest quarters, modest equipment, and modest production activities. This book does not pretend or presume to be an operating manual, a maintenance manual, or a repair manual for TV equipment. Those are best obtained—and translated—by the manufacturer selling the equipment.

Third, the extraordinary explosion of interest in communications over the last two decades shows no sign of abating, nor has it peaked on the college and high school level. For example, when I established the communications department at Hofstra University some dozen years ago, we attracted almost 400 majors within the first 18 months of its existence, making it almost instantly the second largest department in our college. As color TV equipment becomes more compact, more rugged, cheaper to buy and to maintain, and more amenable to operating in marginal light, many additional colleges, high schools, junior high schools, and even elementary schools will get into modest TV studio operations.

The word "Preface" implies something that is "written beforehand." That is not the case with this book. If anything, "Epilogue" might be more appropriate in that this book "evolved" more than it was "written." It is the product of my having taught literally hundreds of college classes in television production over the last quarter of a century. I hope to have compiled the book that I wish I could have had all these years.

Fred Allen once said: "Television is the ultimate triumph of equipment over talent!" As with most aphorisms, there is a germ of truth in the statement—but only a germ. It was not the quill pen that made Shakespeare a great writer. He probably would have done as well with a typewriter or word processor. TV equipment is the instrument; the use to which it is put is what counts. If this book succeeds in demystifying some of the equipment and procedures involved in TV production for the potential practitioner or just the consumer of TV, it will have served much of its purpose.

ACKNOWLEDGMENTS

I am indebted to the generations of students in my Introduction to TV Production classes who have helped me distill from the experience of hundreds of such classes what the beginning student needs and wants to know about TV production, what dosage is appropriate, and over what period of time it should be administered in order to avoid overdose—or underdose—and to make it "pleasant tasting."

I am indebted to a number of Long Island High School coordinators of television for sharing with me their instructional methods and lending their counsel about what sort of text is needed for beginning TV production students. Among these are: Herbert Deutsch of Herricks High, John Collins of Mineola High, Karen Donnelly and John Martz of Hauppauge High, and Robert Gluck of Great Neck South Middle School.

I am indebted to the authors of the TV production books listed in the bibliography—each of whom, in turn, benefited from previous ones, apparently seeing no need to reinvent the wheel.

I am indebted to Cablevision Program Services of Woodbury, New York, particularly to Irene McPhail and Tom Garger, for their generous assistance in obtaining the excellent photographs of equipment in use at their production center.

I am indebted to the equipment manufacturers for their promptness and generosity in providing photographs of their latest equipment, with ample explanatory material. These include: Beaveronics, Inc.; Cetec Vega; Colortran, Inc.; Davis & Sanford Company; Electro-Voice, Inc.; HM Electronics Inc.; Ikegami; ISI Corporation; Kliegl Brothers; Kroy Industries; Mole-Richardson Co.; Panasonic Corporation; Polaroid Corp.; Quickset; Q-TV of Q-Co. Industries; RCA; Sennheiser Electronic Corp.; Shure Brothers, Inc.; Sony Corporation of America; Swintek Enterprises, Inc.; The Great American Market; and Zeimark Corp.

I am indebted to Linda Prieto for her skill, reliability, and ingenuity in preparing the manuscript, to Patricia Hopkins for the line drawings, and to Francis DiPetris, Peter Dykstra, Leon Hoffman, and Robert Lagarenne for the photographs.

Finally—but mostly—I am indebted to my immediate family, Nancy and Carina, for their encouragement and for their forbearance when I was less than charming company, and to our two dogs. Bernie and Bobby, who, on the several occasions when I overlooked taking them for their walks, made no complaint.

Understanding Television Production

1
THE AUDIO PERSON

Essentially, the audio person's function is to deal with various aspects of sound in the studio in advance of the actual program presentation, as well as in the control room shortly before and during the actual broadcast.

STUDIO ACTIVITIES

With regard to beforehand studio activities, one of the first duties is to diagnose the audio needs of the program and to select the appropriate microphones. The function of all microphones is to receive sound waves and convert them into electrical energy which is then amplified and converted back into sound waves by a loudspeaker.

Microphone Selection

Important considerations in selecting the microphone include *construction* and *design, sensitivity, fidelity, pattern of pickup,* and proposed *placement* in relation to the sound source. These considerations are not mutually exclusive and tend to overlap. There is no all-purpose, "wonder" microphone suitable for all occasions. The audio person should be familiar with the considerations involved in selecting a mike for a particular show and then weigh these elements according to his or her best judgment.

With regard to construction and design, the *dynamic* (or *pressure*) microphone is a compact, robust, rugged microphone particularly suited to small/medium studios especially in school, nonbroadcast situations, in which budgetary constraints might impose equipment compromises. The dynamic microphone operates by sound wave pressure variations causing a diaphragm to vibrate, thereby causing a small coil of wire to move back and forth within a magnetic field—thereby generating a weak voltage to be amplified later in the control room. The dynamic microphone, despite its limited frequency response which makes it unacceptable to use for music and high fidelity sound, is considered the workhorse, the bread-and-butter microphone, particularly suited to "remote" and "on-location" uses.

The *velocity* (or *ribbon*) microphone is a more fragile instrument. Instead of the incoming sound waves vibrating a diaphragm, as with the dynamic microphone, the velocity microphone vibrates a thin metal ribbon suspended in a magnetic field. Although the velocity microphone is much more sensitive to a wider spectrum of sound than is the dynamic microphone and although it offers a higher fidelity response, its fragility makes it subject to damage or total destruction should it be exposed to physical or acoustic shocks quite common in the TV studio. Its best use is in the high fidelity, highly controlled setting of the recording studio.

The *condenser* microphone operates as sound waves vibrate a diaphragm that comprises one of two plates needed for a condenser to function. As the diaphragm vibrates against the other plate, which is stationary, the capacitance of the condenser is changed, thereby modulating the electrical current. The major advantage of the condenser microphone over the dynamic microphone and the velocity microphone is its sensitivity and wide frequency response, making it ideal for professional, high fidelity uses, such as recording an orchestra. Its major disadvantages include its tendency to distort loud, nearby sounds, its relatively large size, its high cost, its fragility, and the fact that it requires a special power supply and a nearby preamplifier.

With regard to *pick-up patterns,* the audio person should select microphones with an eye (or ear) to the pattern of pick-up most likely to provide the greatest degree of fidelity. The pick-up pattern, a schematic of which is usually provided with the microphone by the manufacturer, is called a *polar pattern,* presumably because it visualizes the area of pick-up as it might be viewed from above. This polar pattern schematic might be misleading to some insofar as it seems to depict a horizontal "slice" of area, whereas in fact the pick-up zone is a three-dimensional area, as high as it is wide. The major patterns of microphone pick-up are *omnidirectional, unidirectional, highly directional,* and *bidirectional.*

The omnidirectional microphone, as the name suggests, picks up

4 *The Audio Person*

sound coming from all directions. (This microphone is sometimes called *nondirectional,* a potentially misleading term insofar as it might suggest that it picks up sound from no direction, a questionable selling point for a microphone!) If one were to picture the pick-up pattern as an orange with the microphone in its center, all sounds created within the sphere at equal distance from the microphone would be picked up equally well, regardless of location within the sphere of pick-up.

The unidirectional microphone (usually called a *cardioid* micro-

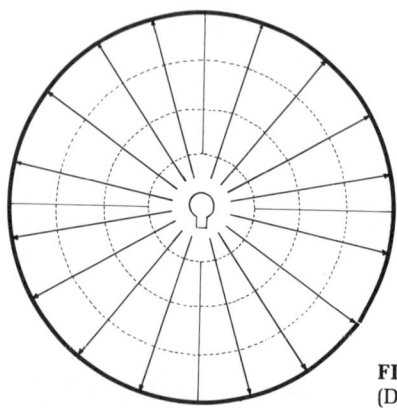

FIGURE 1-1. Omnidirectional Pick-up. (Drawing by Patricia Hopkins.)

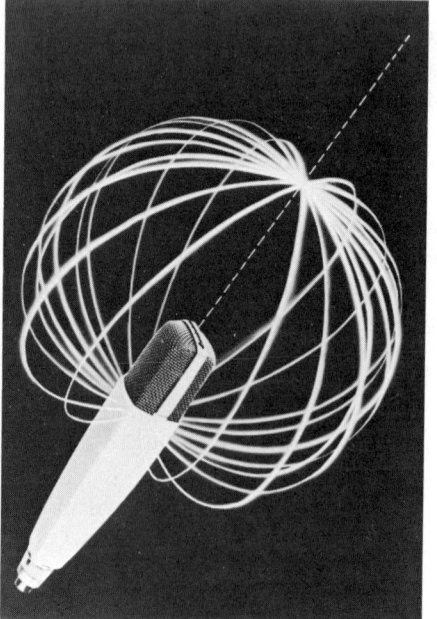

FIGURE 1-2. Omnidirectional Pick-up. (Courtesy of the Sennheiser Electronic Corp.)

phone) does a better job of picking up sound that is directly in front of it, less of an effective job with sound in front and to the side of it, and a poor job with sound behind the microphone. One might picture the pick-up pattern like an upside-down apple, wherein all sounds would be picked-up.

The highly directional microphone (sometimes called the *supercardioid* microphone) exaggerates and elongates the pattern of pick-up so that one might picture the pattern as a pear, wherein all sounds would be picked-up.

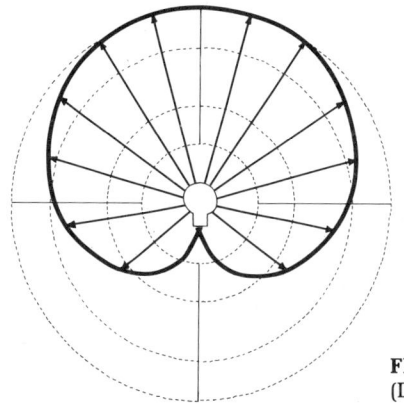

FIGURE 1-3. Unidirectional Pick-up. (Drawing by Patricia Hopkins.)

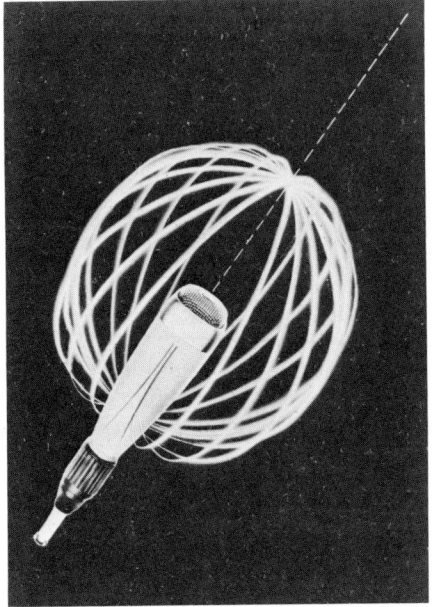

FIGURE 1-4. Unidirectional Pick-up. (Courtesy of the Sennheiser Electronic Corp.)

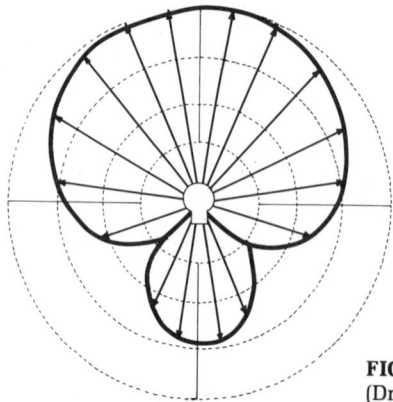

FIGURE 1-5. Supercardioid Pick-up. (Drawing by Patricia Hopkins.)

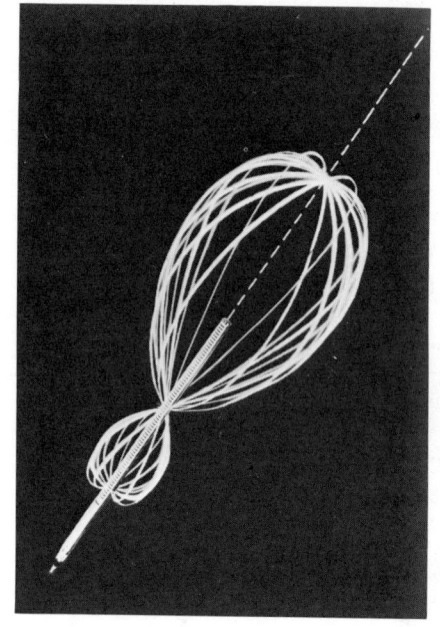

FIGURE 1-6. Supercardioid Pick-up. (Courtesy of the Sennheiser Electronic Corp.)

    The bidirectional microphone picks up sound from the front and the back equally well but not from the sides. Its pick-up pattern might be visualized as a horizontal hour-glass. This type of pick-up is especially suitable for use in radio in that it enables performers to face each other and still be "on mike," thereby increasing rapport. Except for some occasional use in musical programs, this feature is of little value in TV programs.

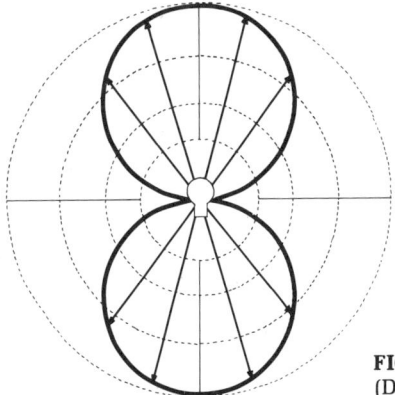

FIGURE 1-7. Bidirectional Pick-up. (Drawing by Patricia Hopkins.)

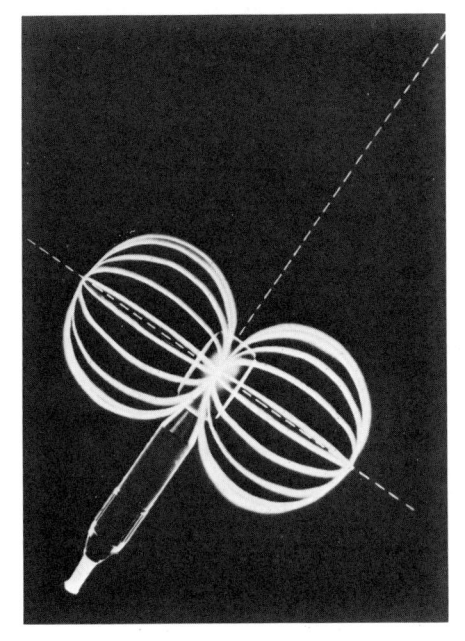

FIGURE 1-8. Bidirectional Pick-up. (Courtesy of the Sennheiser Electronic Corp.)

Mounting and Placement

Having considered the design, fidelity, and pick-up pattern in selecting microphones, the audio person must consider how they should be mounted and placed with relation to the program being contemplated. Although the categories overlap, these are the major categories of microphone mounting and usage: *stationary, moveable,* and *personal* microphones.

Stationary microphones, used when the talent is not expected to move about, include desk, floorstand, and hanging microphones. In actuality programs such as news, interviews, and some discussions—there is no reason to conceal the mikes. In fact, their presence can add a note of "realness" to the situation. Desk mikes are usually at a fixed height so proper placement becomes important. With a newscaster, for example, the microphone should be placed so it does not block the camera view of his or her face even when there are changes in camera angle and in head movement. Care should be taken to avoid extraneous noises being picked-up by the desk microphone—such as the bumping of the desk by the performer's leg, the drumming of fingers on the desk top, and so forth. This can be accomplished by the floor person requesting that the talent stop and/or by placing a felt cloth over the desk top or by placing a carpet square of matching color under the desk mike itself. Should several desk mikes be needed, they should be of the same type lest they cause adjustment problems for the audio person. Microphone cables should be inconspicuous and should be secured by wrapping them around the table leg and taping them to the table and to the floor to prevent the microphone's being pulled off the table accidentally.

Floorstand, omnidirectional microphones are adjustable in height and can be effective for large groups of people or for orchestras, providing the volume levels of the voices or the instruments do not contrast too much. The best use of floorstand microphones is for off-camera announcers and narrators.

The *hanging* microphone is best used in picking-up large groups, such as orchestras, but it can be difficult to position so as to be close enough to pick-up the sounds and yet not so close as to be seen in the picture when a long shot is taken by the camera. Also, its use imposes an additional burden on performers if they have to worry about moving out of the microphone's pick-up pattern. The hanging mike's main advantage is that it eliminates the need for the bulky boomlike apparatus and its microphone cables—a valuable advantage, especially in an already cluttered small studio.

Most of the microphones used in TV production today are moveable—that is to say, they can move during the program as the talent moves. The most widely used types of mounting for a moveable microphone are the *boom* mike and the *shotgun* mike. Going from the largest, most complex and most versatile to the least, these include the *big boom*, the *medium-sized perambulator boom*, the *giraffe boom* and the *fishpole boom*.

The perambulator boom is much too cumbersome and too ex-

FIGURE 1-9. Perambulator Boom: Can be moved around in the studio; operator's platform height is variable; boom arm can be extended, retracted, moved vertically or horizontally; microphone (not pictured) can be rotated. (Courtesy of Mole-Richardson Co., Hollywood, California.)

pensive and requires two men to operate so it will not be considered here except for inclusion of a photograph.

The giraffe boom is mounted on a lightweight tripod which gives it maximum flexibility and therefore maximum studio coverage if properly operated. It can be panned and tilted, the microphone proper can be rotated to face any direction, and it can be moved from one area of the studio to another without great effort or delay. The problems encountered in the use of the giraffe boom are: since, unlike the larger booms, its arm can only be extended easily *before* the program begins, the entire unit must be moved to follow the action; it becomes top-heavy when the arm is extended too far; it runs into other microphone cables, into camera cables, and into the floor person's cable; it can cast unanticipated boom shadows. (See Figure 1-10.)

The simplest, smallest, most flexible and cheapest boom is the fishpole boom microphone, but it needs an operator. Attached to an 8-foot-long aluminum or bamboo pole (as the name suggests), it is a microphone in a shockproof, noise-insulated cradle. The major problem in its use is that it is heavy and awkward to operate, even for short intervals.

The second major type of moveable mike is the highly directional

FIGURE 1-10. Giraffe Boom. (Photograph by Francis De Pretis.)

shotgun microphone which can be mounted on a boom or hand-held with a pistol-grip. It is used when a long reach for sound and a narrow field of acceptance is involved, such as for audience questions at a press conference. Most shotgun mikes are about 2 feet long but the "machine-gun" version is about 8 feet long.

Personal microphones—those which are handled or worn by the talent—include *hand-held* microphones, *lavalier* microphones, and *wireless* microphones.

Hand-held microphones are omnidirectional and are especially appropriate for use in situations in which the talent controls the sound pick-up, as might the M.C. in an audience participation show. Since no pretense is made that no microphone is used—unlike in drama where the mike is concealed—the M.C. can position it as close as necessary to the person he or she is speaking with. The hand-held microphone, in the hand of a singer skilled in its use, can provide an additional element in interpreting the lyrics and the music, as Judy Garland so ably demonstrated. The disadvantages of the hand-held microphone include the fact the quality of sound pick-up is not as good as with a boom microphone and that the microphone cable might get in the way of things, and might limit movement by the talent to some degree.

FIGURE 1-11. Hand-held, Wireless Microphone: Model 81 transmitter with Shure SM58 dynamic element. (Courtesy of Cetec Vega.)

FIGURE 1-12. Lavalier Microphone: Clip-on type, Model ECM-50 PBW. (Courtesy of Sony Corporation of America.)

FIGURE 1-13. Table of Microphones.

Manufacturer/Model #		Type	Pick-up Pattern	Uses and Characteristics
Electro-voice CO94	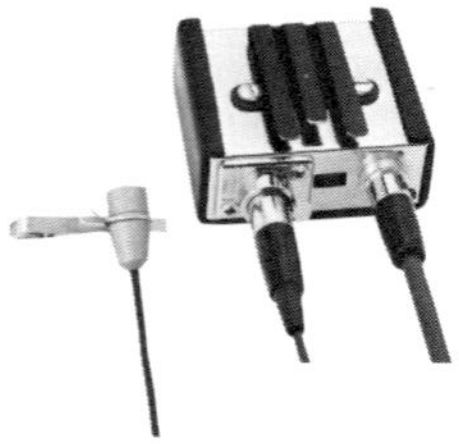	Miniature Electret Condenser	Omnidirectional	Tiny lavalier attached to clasp connected to belt-clip power supply, offers advantages resulting from barrier reinforcement when wall or floor mounted.
Electro-voice 649B		Miniature Dynamic	Omnidirectional	Extremely rugged lavalier can be hand-held or stand mounted, good for audience participation shows, panels, interviews where mobility, inconspicuousness, and free movement of hands desired.
Shure SM11		Miniature Dynamic	Omnidirectional	Versatile, lightweight lavalier with tie bar and tie tack assembly and connector belt clip, excellent frequency response.

Shure 545L — Dynamic — Unidirectional — Bulkier and heavier than most lavaliers but excellent voice reproduction, minimizes feedback, mountable on gooseneck or swivel adaptor.

Sony ECM-50PBW — Condenser — Omnidirectional — Tiny, lightweight, nonreflective version of ECM-50 PS lavalier, excellent quality measures $7/16$" by $13/16$" and weighs 0.3 oz., uses either battery or phantom power source.

Sennheiser MD421 — Dynamic — Unidirectional — Superb directionality and freedom from overload, wide frequency response, rugged construction, resistant to interference from stray magnetic fields.

Electro-voice RE55 — Dynamic — Omnidirectional — Ideal for boom or stand mounting or hand use, smooth wide range response, sturdy construction despite sleek style.

Electro-voice 664A	Dynamic	Supercardioid	Excellent for quality recording, filters out unwanted sound, allows close-in speech without booming.
Electro-voice RE20	Dynamic	Cardioid	Specially suited to recording requiring flat response over wide frequency range, integral blast and wind filter eliminates "p-pops" and extra sibilance.
Sennheiser MD 441	Dynamic	Supercardioid	Durable, top-of-the-line, very wide, smooth frequency response, built-in grill/windscreen, low handling noise.
Shure SM58	Dynamic	Unidirectional	General purpose for speech, instruments, and especially vocalists since windscreen permits close-mike use; hand-held, desk, or floorstand use.

Microphone	Type	Polar Pattern	Description
Shure SM53	Dynamic	Cardioid	Extremely rugged, general use quality microphone, can be hand-held or mounted on stand or desk holder.
Sennheiser MD 431	Dynamic	Supercardioid	Rugged, heavy-duty with double wall construction reduces handling and other vibrations, eliminates unwanted sounds from side and back.
RCA 77DX	Ribbon	Cardioid/variable	Traditional, floorstand mike still used for quality speech and music recording, switch changes polar pattern pick-up.
Electro-voice 635A	Dynamic	Omnidirectional	High output level and low sensitivity to mechanical shock make it excellent for interviews for pass-around use in audience participation shows and for hand-held use by vocalists.

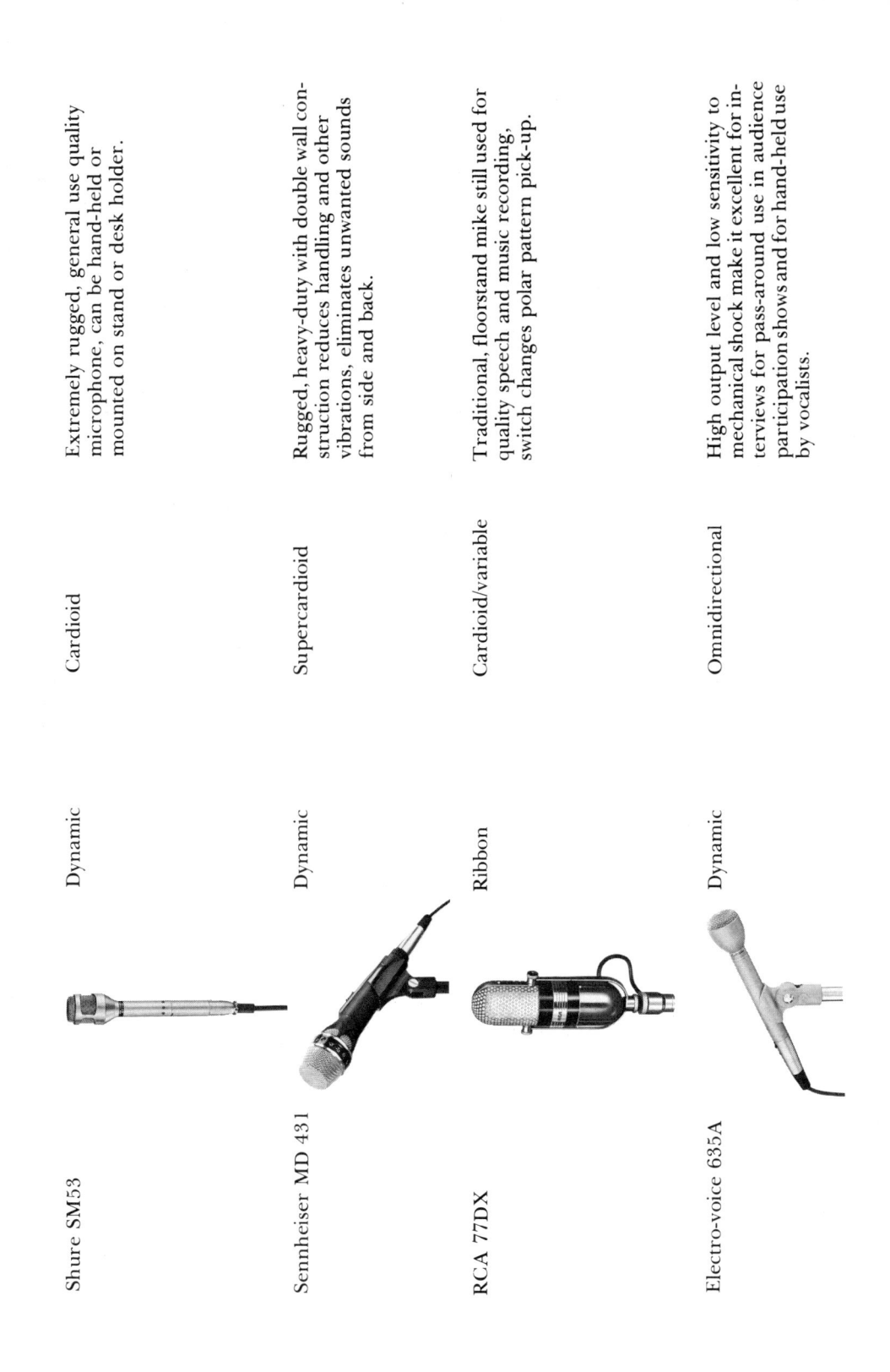

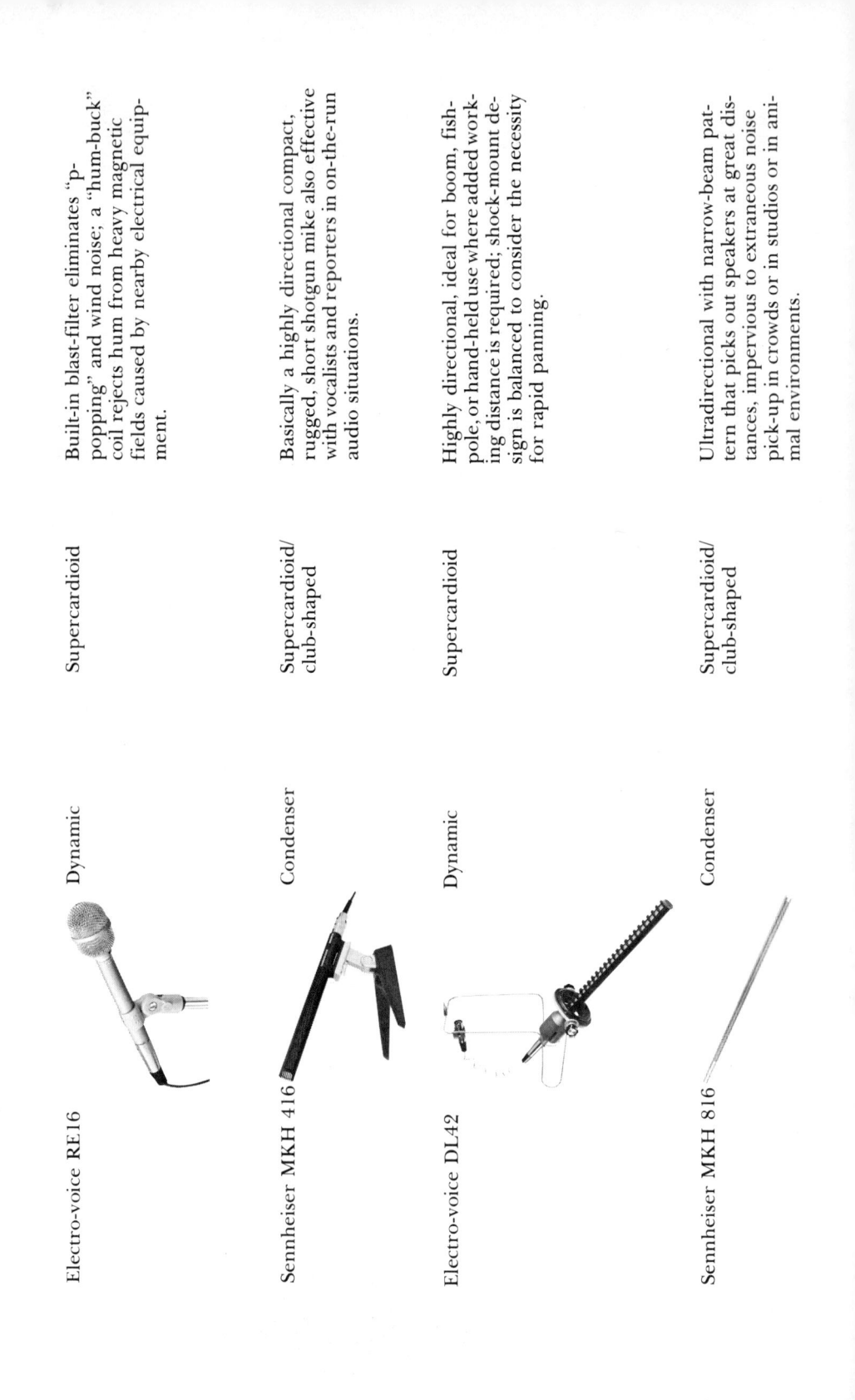

Electro-voice RE16 — Dynamic — Supercardioid — Built-in blast-filter eliminates "p-popping" and wind noise; a "hum-buck" coil rejects hum from heavy magnetic fields caused by nearby electrical equipment.

Sennheiser MKH 416 — Condenser — Supercardioid/club-shaped — Basically a highly directional compact, rugged, short shotgun mike also effective with vocalists and reporters in on-the-run audio situations.

Electro-voice DL42 — Dynamic — Supercardioid — Highly directional, ideal for boom, fish-pole, or hand-held use where added working distance is required; shock-mount design is balanced to consider the necessity for rapid panning.

Sennheiser MKH 816 — Condenser — Supercardioid/club-shaped — Ultradirectional with narrow-beam pattern that picks out speakers at great distances, impervious to extraneous noise pick-up in crowds or in studios or in animal environments.

Sennheiser Telemike — Variable — Variable — Modular multimike system offers omnidirectional, supercardioid, shotgun, spot, and lavalier patterns of pick-up depending on which of five heads is attached to powering module equipped with battery or remote controlled phantom circuit.

Vega 775 transmitter 63 receiver — Dynamic — Omnidirectional — Dual diversity, wireless, uses two antennas each feeding an independent receiver section with diversity combiner circuit which automatically (electronically) switches to the stronger of two signals, thereby eliminating fades and dropouts; because transmitter operates in the VHF high band unwanted radio interference is lessened; range up to 1000 ft.

Vega 82, with Shure SM 58 dynamic element — Condenser — Cardioid — Hand-held wireless, self-contained transmitter, battery and antenna, especially suitable for vocalists; range up to 1000 ft.

HME System 25, with Shure SM58 dynamic element — Dynamic — Cardioid — Hand-held wireless mike with concealed antenna.

(Courtesy: Cetec Vega Inc.; Electro-Voice; HM Electronics, Inc.; RCA; Sennheiser Electronic Corp.; Shure Bros. Inc.; Sony Corp.)

The lavalier microphone has been a boon to TV production. The larger lavalier microphone, about the size of a man's thumb, is fastened to a necklace-like cord that goes around the neck. The smaller lavalier microphone, about the size of a man's thumbnail, is usually clipped to a tie or a shirt or a lapel. The main advantages of the lavalier microphone include the fact that, since the distance between the performer's mouth and the microphone remains relatively constant, adjustments of volume by the audio person in the control room are less necessary. Further, they do not cause boom shadows; unlike a hand-held microphone, the performer's hands are free; and unlike using a boom microphone, the performer need not worry about falling "off mike." The main shortcomings include the fact that the performer cannot get closer to it or further from it should he or she choose to; also, since it must remain exposed to view to operate at its best, it cannot be used in dramatic scenes; quality of pick-up cannot equal that of boom mikes; and the performer may feel tethered by the cable. (Incidentally, dual-lavalier clip-on microphones have come into vogue, perhaps because of the 22-minute audio-gap during the Carter-Ford presidential debate when the world waited while an audio person scurried frantically for a new lavalier microphone when Carter's microphone went out.)

Another type of personal microphone is the *wireless* (or FM) microphone. Essentially, this is a miniature lavalier-type microphone attached to a concealed belt (or pocket) transmitter or sometimes a large lavalier or hand-held microphone with a built-in transmitter. A special receiver picks up the signal (from as far as 1200 feet away) and feeds it to the audio mixer. The *Donahue* show provides an excellent example of the use of a hand-held wireless FM microphone. The main advantages of the wireless microphone include the fact that it eliminates the need for microphone cable and allows for complete freedom of movement—an especially valuable feature for officials at football games, for people walking outdoors, for stage actors, and so forth. The main problems encountered with its use are: technically an FCC license is required to use an FM frequency; each such wireless FM microphone needs its own transmitter and receiver (raising the possibility of interference between them); quality of sound pick-up might not be as good as with a regular mike; these units are relatively expensive to buy and to maintain; and the FM signal might be distorted by nearby electronic equipment, including the TV equipment itself. All factors considered, the wireless FM microphone may not be practical for use in the small/medium TV studio, although these mikes lend valuable assistance on remote broadcasts done in the field.

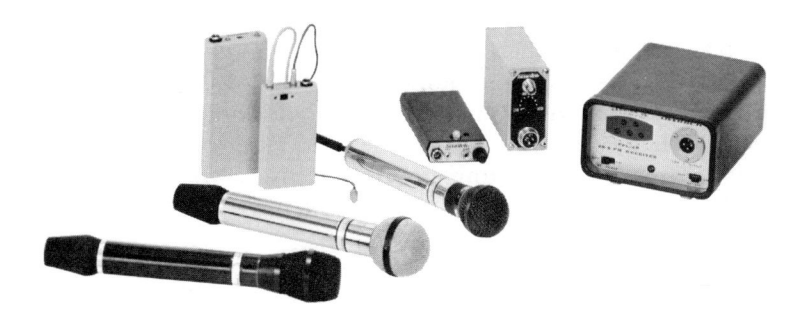

FIGURE 1-14. Wireless Microphones: Hand-held and lavalier models, transmitters, and receivers. (Courtesy of Swintek.)

Cables and Connections

Having diagnosed the audio needs of a production, having chosen the appropriate microphones, and having considered microphone mounting and placement, the audio person must connect the microphones by cable to the wall plugs which, in turn, are connected to the audio console he or she will operate later in the control room. In this regard, the audio person will need to be familiar with these considerations and be able to cope with them: *lo-and-hi impedance, balanced* and *unbalanced* lines, and *audio plugs*.

Impedance is a characteristic of such electronic devices as microphones, audio inputs, and audio outputs. Impedance refers to a type of resistance to the flow of electronic audio signals through a microphone cable. The main thing for an audio person to know is that only audio inputs and audio outputs that match in impedance should be put together or energy loss will result and sometimes frequency loss as well. High impedance (sometimes shortened to *HI Z*, when Z stands for impedance) microphones produce a stronger electrical signal; however, because the signal encounters greater resistance, HI Z mikes work well with shorter cables only—cables less than 15 feet long, usually 8 feet long. Smaller installations are more likely to use HI Z equipment than are professional TV set-ups. Because low impedance (*LO Z*) audio equipment produces a lower output audio signal, it can travel further in the cable—several hundred feet if necessary. Low impedance devices work better in a high impedance input than high impedance devices work in a low impedance input, but quality is best achieved by components with matching impedance. Should the audio person be forced to mix HI Z and LO Z components, an impedance matching transformer—which transforms the one type of electronic signal into the other—may be required. The type of impedance of a microphone is printed on the microphone. Professional microphones often have a HI/LO Z switch. Frequently microphone inputs specify the impedance involved in the unit and frequently microphone mixers and amplifiers are equipped with HI/LO Z switches to make a compatible connection.

With regard to balanced and unbalanced lines, the cable carrying the audio signal from the microphone to the wall socket does that in one of two ways: through a balanced line or an unbalanced line. The balanced line contains two center wires to carry the audio signal with a braided outside shield. Since balanced lines are of higher quality, they carry audio signals over longer distances without picking up extraneous electrical interference from nearby sources. Balanced lines normally are found with quality professional equipment and are associated with the higher quality, LO Z microphone and related equipment. The unbalanced line contains only one center wire and an outside shield which also carries part of the audio signal. This factor makes it more susceptible to stray interference and makes it necessary to limit sharply the length of the cable carrying the audio signal. Unbalanced lines are used with HI Z microphones. The potential electronic interference can be minimized by not laying microphone cables near other power cables or, if that is not possible, by having them cross those cables at right angles rather than having them run parallel. Except for this interference, unbalanced lines are adequate for most small/medium studio uses and are especially suitable because ½" and ¾" video equipment do not operate with balanced lines. The manufacturers of HI Z microphones provide the longest suitable cables for their microphones. It should be noted that 1"-video equipment accepts audio signals from balanced lines, however.

Microphone Plugs

With regard to *audio plugs,* the most common types in use are the Cannon company plug, known as the *XLR* plug, usually found at the end of a balanced line, and the *mini plug,* the *phone plug,* and the *RCA* (or phono) *plug,* all three of which are usually found at the end of unbalanced lines. These plugs are designed to fit into openings of the same size and shape, called *jacks.* When the plug does not fit the jack into which the microphone is to be plugged, an adaptor (or an adaptor cable assembly) is needed. There are literally hundreds of combinations of plugs, adaptors, adaptor cables, and jacks—too many to go into here. Suffice it to say that when the desired combination of plug and jack is not available, technicians are called upon to solder appropriate adaptors to effect the proper fit.

Cannon plugs are the heavy-duty plugs usually employed to connect the studio microphones into a numbered studio receptacle found spaced at various intervals around the studio or bunched up in one junction box location. The next link between studio and control room with regard to audio is the patch bay. In most small/medium studios the audio line from the studio is permanently wired into the console ("normalled"). If it is not, a unit in the control room known as the patch bay enables the audio person, like a telephone operator, to connect the numbered output in the patch bay that corresponds to the receptacle in the studio (into which a particular microphone is plugged) directly into the audio console and to the appropriate controls for that sound source.

FIGURE 1-15. Studio Junction Box. (Courtesy of Cablevision Systems Development Co.)

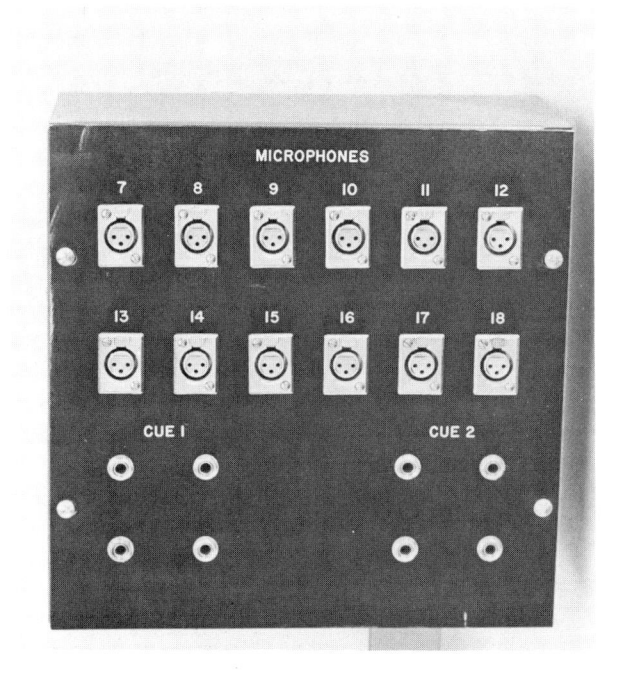

FIGURE 1-16. Audio Patch Bay, shown here attached to an audio cartridge unit. (Photograph by Peter Dykstra.)

FIGURE 1-17. Audio Patch Bay, shown here as part of a unit including reel-to-reel tape recorder and audio cartridge unit. (Photograph by Robert Lagarenne.)

CONTROL ROOM ACTIVITIES

In a small/medium TV installation, the four major pieces of equipment with which the audio person is involved while in the control room—as opposed to the studio—are the *audio console,* the *turntable,* the *audiotape recorder,* and the *audio cartridge recorder.*

Audio Console

The audio console—whether it be the modest version to be described here or the elaborate professional audio control board shown here for comparison purposes—is intended to accept and to mix (blend) the various incoming sources of sound, whether these sounds come from microphones, records, prerecorded tapes and cartridges, or whatever. As indicated previously, studio microphones are plugged into wall sockets in the studio which are, unless permanently wired from studio microphone inputs to the audio console, then connected by a "patch cord" to the audio console. Each microphone in use accepts the sound

FIGURE 1-18. Audio Console equipped with rotary knobs. (Photograph by Robert Lagarenne.)

FIGURE 1-19. Audio Console: Professional quality. (Courtesy of Cablevision Systems Development Co.)

being made, whether it be speech, music, or sound effects, but the signal is weak and needs to be boosted by a pre-amplifier. Other sound sources—such as audiotape recorders and turntables—are equipped with built-in pre-amplifiers so their signal can go directly to the overall program amplifier. Controlling the *input* of each microphone or other sound source is an input selector switch that has three positions: *cue, off,* and *program*. When the switch is thrown to the cue position, the audio person can "preview" what the microphone is going to pick-up before it is actually used in the program. This same position is used to cue records. The middle position, off, is self-explanatory. The program position is used to put the sound into the program, either on-the-air or on the videotape recording. In addition to this input switch, each microphone is controlled by its own rotary knob (or *pot,* for potentiometer) which regulates the volume of the audio current. It is operated much like the volume control on a radio receiver. When in its closed position, the pot's white-line indicator is in a position analogous to the numeral 7 on the face of a clock or watch. As the rotary knob is turned clockwise, (or *on*), current is allowed to pass through and this process is known as *fading up* the sound. Conversely, when the knob is turned counterclockwise, less current is allowed to pass through and this process is called *fading down* the sound.

The audio person's responsibilities include maintaining the appropriate level of volume on all such individual inputs and on their combination, a process known as *riding gain*. On some audio consoles the knobs are replaced by *slide-faders*. Fading up is accomplished by

FIGURE 1-20. Input Selector Switch in OFF position, between *audition* (or *cue*) and *program* position. Below: *rotary knob* (or *pot*). (Photograph by Robert Lagarenne.)

pushing the slide-fader up and fading down by pulling the slide-fader down. Among the advantages of the slide-fader over the rotary knob is the fact that the audio person can tell at a glance which microphones are open and relatively by how much; also several slide-faders can be manipulated more easily than an equivalent number of rotary knobs.

The output of each sound source—whether it be a microphone that needs a pre-amplifier or whether it be a turntable that has a built-in pre-amplifier—plus the total composite signal goes to a program amplifier in the audio console. This program amplifier again increases the audio energy and feeds it through a *volume unit (VU) meter,* sometimes called a *volume indicator (VI)*. The VU meter enables the audio person to visually balance not only the intensity of each individual sound source but also to control the composite, overall output by using a master pot. The VU meter shows a dual scale. The lower scale shows the volume units (decibels) from −20 to 0 and then to +3, marked in red. The upper scale is marked from left to right, from 0 to 100, indicating the percentage of modulation, 100 percent being ideal. The needle of the VU meter oscillates according to volume variations of the overall product of the inputs. If the needle hovers around the −20 point (or the 0 percent of the upper scale), incoming volume level is too low. If it peaks over 0 (100 percent on the upper scale) and thereby into the red too often the level is too high and the sound will be distorted and, if maintained high enough long enough, equipment

FIGURE 1-21. Slide Faders being operated on an audio console. (Courtesy of Cablevision Systems Development Co.)

might be damaged. The audio person, in "riding gain," should try to keep the needle hovering about the middle of the scales, allowing perhaps an occasional "kick" into the red zone. The process is done for each of the pots (or slide-faders) *first* and then it is done for the composite overall signal by using the master pot.

Audio Turntable

The audio turntable is the next control room item of equipment with which the audio person is involved. The turntable consists of a large, sturdy, flat revolving disk covered with rubber or felt, which sits atop a cabinet containing a heavy-duty motor and large flywheel to provide smooth and rapid engagement of the gears; this engagement allows smooth and consistent operation of the turntable. Somewhere near the

FIGURE 1-22. Volume Unit Meters. (Photograph by Robert Lagarenne.)

FIGURE 1-23. Audio Turntable. (Photograph by Robert Lagarenne.)

turntable plate is the *on/off* switch and the *speed selector* switch, which determines whether the unit will play records at 33⅓ RPM (revolutions per minute), 78 RPM, or 45 RPM. Next to the plate is a pick-up arm which contains a playback cartridge and the needle. The needle (stylus) picks up the mechanical vibrations caused by the grooves of the record so that the cartridge can convert this mechanical vibration into electrical vibration. Thus, the pick-up arm becomes the link between the record and the control console. Very often the control room console is equipped with filter/equalizers which enable the audio person not only to control the volume of the sound but also to "shape" the sound. Filtering out high frequencies can eliminate the scratch of old records. Equalizers can enable the audio person to simulate such effects as the other end of a telephone conversation, echoes, and so forth, for dramatic programs.

One of the functions of the audio person using a turntable is to "cue up" a record at a precise starting point so that it will come up precisely when called for by the director. Cueing up a record is done with the use of a small cue speaker or, to avoid adding to the noise in the control room or to avoid being distracted by the noise, through the use of headphones. The procedure for cueing up a record is as follows:

1. Set the selector speed switch to the appropriate speed for the record being cued.
2. Put the pot into the cue (or audition) position, which is all the way to the left on the rotary knob type of pot or the bottom location if the pot is of the slide-fade variety.
3. Turn the knob on and play the record until you locate the exact spot on the record you want to hear. Some audio persons prefer to rotate the turntable top manually instead of turning on the motor to have the plate rotate. Most turntables are equipped with a felt layer that allows the record and felt to move independently of each other.
4. As soon as the desired sound is heard, stop the record from rotating by placing the finger of the right hand on the outside edge. Then rotate the record manually in a counterclockwise direction about one-quarter of a turn; this one-quarter revolution is designed to prevent the "wow" going on the air before the turntable has picked up playing speed. The record is now cued up.
5. If use of the sound cue is imminent, the audio person uses his left hand to turn the pot from the cue position to the 0 volume level and then turns on the turntable power. The left hand then holds the pot and the right hand holds the edge of the record so that the turntable platter revolves freely beneath the record and the felt liner. When the director calls for the sound, the right hand releases the record and felt liner and the left hand turns the pot clockwise to the proper level of volume.

These are two situations in which the left hand on pot and the right hand holding the edge of the record while the turntable revolves beneath it will not be practical. The first is when instead of a moveable felt pad the turntable is covered with a fixed, non-skid rubber mat, in which case instead the record must be started from a dead stop and instead of a quarter-turn counterclockwise, a half turn is needed to permit the turntable to come up to playing speed and avoid the "wow." The second situation is when the sound is not needed until sometime after the record has been cued up. In those situations, the turntable is put into neutral with the motor running or the turntable is left in gear but the motor is turned off. Later, when the director calls for the sound either the gearshift is switched to the correct speed slot or the motor is switched on.

It should be noted that the console VU does not monitor any sound when the switch is in the cue position, but only in the program position. Thus, the audio person—when cueing up a sound, has no visual representation of its volume until it already has been broadcast or recorded. Thus, volume levels should be checked before actual production time, and proper volume settings should be marked on the knobs of slide-fader to reduce guesswork, fumbling, and delay.

In addition to cueing records, the audio person is charged with the proper mixing of prerecorded music. For this, two turntables are necessary. They are operated simultaneously to accomplish such audio effects as *fade, cross-fade,* and *segue.* A fade in is the gradual introduction of a sound source and a fade out is the gradual removal of a sound source. These are accomplished by turning the rotary knob dial clockwise or counterclockwise, respectively, or by raising or lowering the slide-fader. A cross-fade means fading in one record gradually while another record is still playing and then, at the right creative moment, fading in the second record up to full volume and the original record out quickly. A segue (pronounced seg-way) involves having one record follow another without pause, but allowing the first record to play to completion before bringing in the second record, with no overlap.

Audiotape Recorder

Another control room machine with which the audio person is involved is the audiotape recorder. Essentially, the audiotape recorder is a time-saving, labor-saving, and tension-easing device. It allows the audio person to do some of his or her tasks ahead of time. Audio recorder tape is ¼ inch wide, consisting of a thin, magnetic coating on a flexible plastic base. Prior to recording, the audiotape must be magnetically "erased" either totally—through the use of a bulk electromagnetic "eraser"—or as the first part of the re-recording process. The tape recorder's mechanism draws the tape from a supply reel to a take-up

FIGURE 1-24. Audiotape Recorder: Reel-to-reel, table-top model. (Courtesy of Cablevision Systems Development Co.)

reel at a constant speed past several "heads" with which the moving tape comes into contact: the *erase head,* the *record head,* and the *playback head.* When recording, the erase head is encountered first where strong currents remove any previous recording. The "erased" tape next comes into contact with the record head to receive fresh audio information in the form of magnetic patterns on the oxide coating of the tape. During playback, the erase head and the record head are disconnected. The playback head, like the record head, is an electromagnet but it works "backwards"; the magnetic patterns on the recorded tape induce weak voltages in the head, which are then magnified electronically.

All control room audiotape recorders have comparable control buttons to control tape movement, although the order they are arranged in varies from one model to another. *Play* moves the tape at a constant speed from the supply reel to the take-up reel at the speed selected. *Record* activates both the erase head to remove previous recorded material and the record head, which "lays down" the magnetic signal on the oxide side of the tape in the direction of travel of the tape. *Fast forward* activates the tape transport mechanism to advance the tape at high speed. *Stop* brings the tape transport to a quick halt. *Reverse* activates the tape transport mechanism to rewind the tape at an accelerated rate.

In addition to these control buttons, there is a volume control knob (or pot) and a volume meter (VU) to be sure the tape recorder is not overmodulated or undermodulated. There is also a mechanism to determine at what speed the tape will be recorded or played back. Most tape recorders operate at speeds of either 7½ IPS (inches per second) or 3¾ IPS. The higher the speed of the tape the better the frequency response and the better the quality of the sound recorded or played back. The recording industry records its tapes at 15 IPS and even 30 IPS for maximum fidelity and for ease in editing but that involves more tape and therefore larger reels, which might cause some storage problems in the small/medium studio. Although a *monaural* full-track tape contains a track that uses the full width of the tape, more commonly the "half-track" system is used for economy and compactness reasons, both relevant particularly to a small/medium setup. The recording head lays down the magnetic signal on slightly less than ¼ inch of the tape. After the reel has run its course in one direction, the reels are reversed; that is, the take-up reel that is filled with tape becomes the supply reel, and the newly emptied supply reel becomes the take-up reel. The new audio information is then laid down on the blank, unused portion of the tape as the direction of the tape movement is reversed. If *stereo* sound is involved, both halves of the tape are recorded (or played) as the tape is transported in one direction. The tape cannot be reversed (unlike monaural, half-track recording) or the previous recording would be erased. Four-track stereo recording involves using tracks 1 and 3 as tape moves in one direction and tracks 2 and 4 after the reels have been reversed, analogous to the half-track monaural procedure. Although half-track tapes can be played on a one-quarter inch recorder, four-track tapes cannot be played on a half-track machine.

Frequently the audio person is required to edit an audiotape to eliminate errors or to compile a composite tape out of individual segments. One way to edit is to cut and splice. Simply overlap slightly the two ends of tape to be joined, shiny sides up, and cut with a pair of scissors at a 45 degree angle. Next, butt together the cut ends and press adhesive tape to the shiny (plastic) side of the joint. Specially made, pressure sensitive splicing tape should be used rather than ordinary cellophane tape, the adhesive of which would probably run and thereby not only weaken the splice but contaminate other points on the tape as it revolves on the spool. The splicing process can be accomplished with less manual dexterity needed by using a splicing block to hold the two tape ends together in alignment while they are being cut at a 45 degree angle (this time using a razor blade) and the splicing tape is being attached. In either method—the scissors or razor—the cutting instrument should be demagnetized. Most control rooms have a "degauzer" to magnetically "erase" audiotapes and videotapes.

Although the cut and splice method of editing results in a silent joining, it does disturb any recorded material on other tracks of the tape. An alternate method of editing is simply to re-record (dub) the sections you want onto another tape.

When the audio person intends to use separate audio selections during a program, these can more easily be identified if colored, nonmagnetic paper or plastic tape is interspliced as "leader," before the desired section is needed or as silent spaces to separate and identify individual sequences within the tape.

Audiotape Cartridge Machine

The next piece of control room equipment with which the audio person is involved is the audiotape cartridge machine, one of the pieces of audio equipment simplest to understand and operate. The audiotape cartridge is a plastic box containing a looped, continuous, endless audiotape. It automatically rewinds itself as it plays. The audio person simply inserts the cartridge into a slot in the playback machine and presses the *start* button. After the sound has ended the tape continues to roll silently until it reaches a cue tone recorded on a separate track or on the cartridge before the program material, at which point the motion of the tape stops and the cartridge is cued up again for its next use. The cartridge should be allowed to play through the entire loop until the cue tone is reached to turn itself off. If the audio person stops the cartridge prematurely, dead air will result during the next playing of the cartridge. Cartridge machines can be equipped merely to repro-

FIGURE 1-25. Audiotape Cartridge Machine, coupled with turntable. (Courtesy of Cablevision Systems Development Co.)

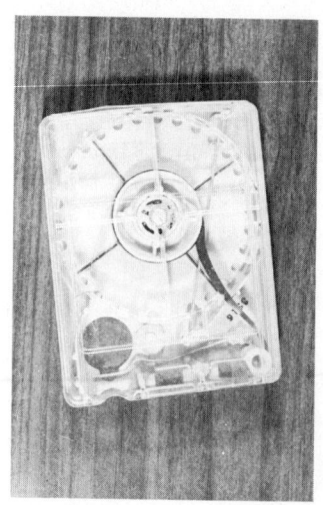

FIGURE 1-26. Audiotape Cartridge. (Photograph by Robert Lagarenne.)

duce already recorded sound or to reproduce already recorded sound and to record fresh sound. Some machines will play up to ten cartridges in any order. Should the audio person want to re-record any program material on a cartridge, the cartridge must be erased first because the machine does not erase while recording new sounds. Cartridges come in lengths from 20 to 150 seconds and from 3½ to 31 minutes. The main advantage of the cartridge machine is that it eliminates the trouble and unpredictability of cueing up prerecorded sounds on records and reel-to-reel tape recordings.

2
THE LIGHTING PERSON

Just as one of the first responsibilities of the audio person is to diagnose the audio needs of the proposed TV program, one of the first responsibilities of the lighting person is to diagnose the lighting needs of the proposed TV programs.

The lighting person should realize that proper lighting is necessary for technical and aesthetic reasons and that these considerations overlap and are by no means actually exclusive. For the sake of simplicity, let us consider the technical aspects and the aesthetic aspects separately.

TECHNICAL ASPECTS OF LIGHTING

Obviously there must be at least a minimum of light to enable the camera to take a respectable picture that will be acceptably visible to the viewer. This is called *baselight*. If the baselight falls below a certain level, the resulting picture will appear snowy, the objects pictured will appear smeary—especially when they move or the camera direction changes; if it is a color picture, the picture colors will be muddy. The simplest way to avoid this would seem to be to flood the entire set with as much light as possible. Apart from the blinding discomfort this would cause for the talent—and apart from the heat it would produce especially in a small/medium TV studio—the resulting picture would be flat, uninteresting, two-dimensional, without contrast—possibly even confusing—and would ignore aesthetic considerations, a treatment of which follows.

In providing at least the minimum light for a technically acceptable picture—the baselight— the lighting person has a choice of two approaches. The first approach would be to establish enough broad and diffused light to fill the entire set and then add individual, more focused lights to emphasize certain elements in the picture to avoid "flat" lighting. The second approach would be to light the more important elements in the picture first and then add more diffused light to bring the overall level to at least the level for a technically acceptable picture. The first method offers the advantage of assuring enough light and consistent light, both especially important in color TV production. It is probably better suited to such objective "reality" programs as newscasts, panel shows, interviews, sports, cooking, and fashion shows, in which the emotional or sensory responses of the audience are not solicited. The second method—lighting the more important elements first and then supplementing enough to create a baselight—is better suited to dramatic, dance, and musical programs.

Although a consideration of the equipment, the hardware, of lighting follows later in this chapter, some mention of the instrument used for measuring light might be injected here.

The lighting person needs to know the overall amount of light on the set—regardless of whether the set is lit first and then the items to be highlighted or vice-versa. To avoid having to depend on the subjective judgment of his or her own eyes, the lighting person employs a light meter which measures the intensity of light coming from the direction

FIGURE 2-1. Lighting person taking *incident light* reading with a light meter. (Courtesy of Cablevision Systems Development Co.)

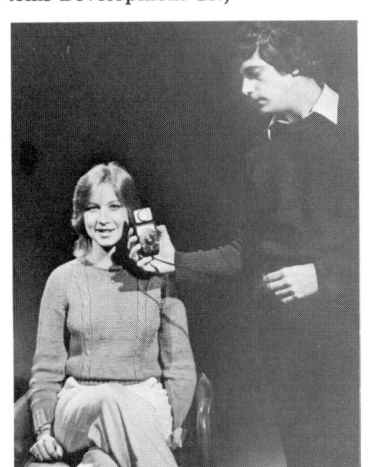

FIGURE 2-2. Lighting person taking *reflective light* reading with a light meter. (Courtesy of Cablevision Systems Development Co.)

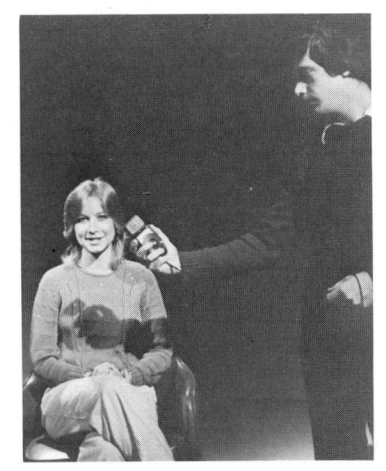

in which it is pointed. The light meter measures the intensity of two types of light: *incident* light and *reflective* light. Incident light measures how much light is coming at the object and is measured by pointing the light meter directly at the light source. Reflective light measures how much light "bounces off" the object and is measured by pointing the meter directly at the object being lit. The lighting person considers both the incident light and the reflective light when computing through the use of the light meter the proper amount of baselight for the particular TV camera to be used.

In addition to the amount of light, the contrast ratio is another technical consideration of concern to the lighting person. Even though the human eye can accommodate—and even distinguish between—items of contrasting brightness of as much as 100 to 1, the TV camera can handle only a contrast range of 20 to 1. The contrast ratio is determined by using the light meter to measure the reflective light of the brightest element in the picture to the darkest element.

Another technical consideration confronting the lighting person is the *color temperature* of white light. Color temperature refers to a scale by which we calibrate the bluish hues and the reddish hues on either end of the color spectrum of white light. Color TV cameras—unlike black and white (B&W) cameras—are sensitive to color temperature. Color temperature is measured by degrees Kelvin, a scale for measuring the actual temperature of a light. The higher the temperature the filament of a lamp gets, the bluer is the light it emits. The lower the temperature filament of a lamp gets, the redder the light it emits. In color TV, the preferred temperature should be within the 3000 K–3200 K range, with a safety margin of about 200 K before discoloring of the picture results, most noticeably on skin tones.

AESTHETIC CONSIDERATIONS

In addition to the technical considerations of providing enough light of appropriate contrast and appropriate color temperature, the lighting person must deal with aesthetic considerations. When we look at something in real life, the fact that our two eyes are separated by about 4 inches enables us to see the object in a three-dimensional, stereoscopic manner. In addition, we are able to move about this object to change our point of view. The TV image is flat and two-dimensional. The angle of view is chosen for us by the director. The viewer sometimes finds it difficult to ascertain the shape, size, and distance of an object or a series of objects. Proper lighting can indicate shape, dimension, distance, and texture. It is through the manipulation of light and its absence—shadows—that viewers can be helped to fathom depth and thereby discern shape, size, texture, and relative distance of the object the camera picks up.

Proper lighting can provide the illusion of reality and, when it is called for, fantasy. Time of day, whether the scene is taking place inside or out, can be communicated by the length and depth of the shadows being cast. The physical setting of the scene can be suggested by off-camera lighting effects—such as a sweeping of light if the scene is taking place in a lighthouse. Shadows cast on the back wall through cutouts might suggest the inside of a church or a prison or a forest. Conversely, proper lighting can provide the illusion of fantasy or nonreality if such is called for. Combined with the electronic manipulation known as reversing polarity, creative lighting can cause the dark portions of a picture to turn light and the light ones to turn dark, thereby causing an eerie effect. Similarly, a silhouette effect can be achieved by lighting so the person remains in darkness but is outlined sharply by a brilliantly lit background. By cameo lighting the person can be lit and the background remains dark to provide an unreal impression.

Proper lighting can establish and heighten the appropriate psychological mood. Low key, dim lighting might generate a sombre, eerie mood while high key, bright lighting might suggest happiness and light-heartedness. The angle of lighting can contribute to psychological mood. For example, lighting a person from below—an unusual, unnatural angle for light—causes a mood of insecurity and mystery. Lighting alone cannot be expected to create and maintain the illusion of reality or of fantasy as well as psychological mood but when combined with other such production elements as set color, music, and sound effects, can make a substantial contribution.

Having considered the objectives and qualities of lighting, let us turn to a consideration of the instruments used in lighting. To do so, some mention should be made of the terms *hard light* and *soft light*. Hard light is highly directional and casts pronounced light areas and relatively few shades in between. The advantage of hard light is that it provides sharp, vigorous, and bold modeling, showing without ambiguity, the shape, size, texture, and spatial relationship of various items in the picture. The disadvantage of hard light is that, since it lacks subtle gradations, it sometimes can be too harsh and crude and can overstress texture, and can stretch the contrast ratio beyond the acceptable range. Soft light is diffused, generally shadowless illumination which provides subtle, half-tone values and gradual shading. Its main advantage is that it can eliminate shadows, can insure that there will be no underlit areas, and can reduce the contrast ratio. The main disadvantage is that it scatters, is not easily restricted, and it can create flat, characterless lighting, reducing shape, form, texture, and spatial relationships.

STUDIO LIGHTS

Let us turn to a consideration of the instruments that provide the illumination in a studio. Perhaps the best way to proceed would be to discuss *bulbs, housings,* and *supports.*

Light Sources: Bulbs

The four major types of light sources to be found in small/medium TV studios are: the regular *tungsten* lamp, the *over-run* lamp, the *quartz* lamp, and the *fluorescent* lamp.

The regular tungsten lamp (commonly called the incandescent, the type used in households) is still in wide use in TV studios and has several advantages: it's cheap to buy, has relatively long life, has a wide variety of intensities, and fits a wide range of TV lighting fixtures. The disadvantages include the fact that tungsten lamps waste much electrical energy as heat; also, as they get older they deteriorate appreciably insofar as the light level of the filament drops, the bulb interior blackens, and the color quality changes.

Over-run lamps are purposely designed to give high intensity light by accepting voltages beyond which the filament was designed. While this increased light and higher color quality is an asset, the working life of these bulbs is sharply curtailed and they are prone to breakdowns—both shortcomings which are especially relevant to the small/medium studio.

Quartz lamps (tungsten-halogen lamps) feature a tungsten filament encased in a quartz bulb containing halogen gas, thus reducing bulb discoloration. Some advantages of this bulb are: it provides twice as much light as an incandescent bulb of the same wattage; it maintains constant, consistent light intensity and color quality throughout its life span; and it is small and lightweight. Some disadvantages are: they last half as long as incandescent bulbs; they get much hotter than incandescent bulbs (an especially undesirable feature in a small/medium TV studio); and this extreme heat is destructive to scrims, gels, and barn doors of lighting instruments.

Fluorescent tubes can be an effective means of economically providing soft light in B&W studios because they have long life and high efficiency, but fluorescent light is of low intensity and its nondirectional quality makes it difficult to harness. Other drawbacks are the bulkiness and fragility of the fluorescent tubes, as well as the fact that the color quality of the light they produce is poorly suited to color TV production.

Studio Lights: Housings

The major categories of studio lighting instruments are the *spotlight* and the *floodlight*. The spotlight provides directional, hard lighting, and the floodlight provides diffused soft light. (It should be noted that some spotlights can be made to provide diffused light and floodlights can be made to provide directional lighting if placed close enough to the subject.)

The two major types of spotlight are the *Fresnel* spotlight and the *ellipsoidal* spotlight. The Fresnel (pronounced without the "s" sound) is the most versatile spotlight and is so widely used in TV that the name "Fresnel" has come to refer to any spotlight of this type regardless of manufacturer, much like the brand name Kleenex has almost become a generic term. Two unique features of the fresnel may account for its versatility: the fresnel lens and its spot-focusing mechanism. The fresnel lens' distinctive structure consists of concen-

FIGURE 2-3. Fresnel Spotlight. (Courtesy of Colortran, Inc.)

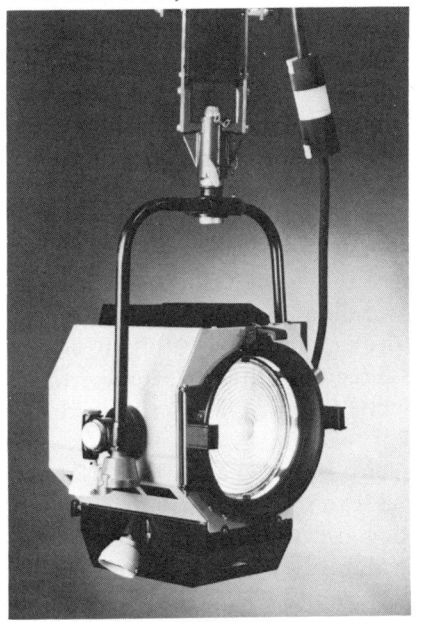

FIGURE 2-4. Ellipsoidal Light: Zoom design provides hard or soft light. (Courtesy of Colortran, Inc.)

tric, grooved steps within the lens which have the same curvature as a regular convex lens of the same diameter, but which cut the weight and bulk of the lens. The fresnel's spot-focusing option allows for adjustment to a sharp, clearly outlined light beam (called a *pinned beam*) by moving the bulb reflector away from the lens to the spotlight position. The option also allows for the adjustment to a diffused, scattered light beam (called the *spread* beam) by moving the bulb reflector away from the lens to the floodlight position. The mechanism for moving the bulb reflector toward or away from the lens may be a spindle, a ring, or a knob that moves horizontally from spotlight to floodlight position.

The second major type of spotlight is the ellipsoidal spotlight, which is used less often and less widely in TV production; its use generally is limited to special effects lighting. This spotlight gives precisely shaped, hard-edged beams of light that can be shaped into a triangle or a rectangle by the use of internal shutters. Some ellipsoidal spotlights can be made to project patterns of decorative shadows on plain backgrounds and, by the addition of metal stencils (called a *cucalorus*, or "cookie") can be made to project such sharp-edged patterns as windows, forests, and so forth.

In contrast to spotlights, which provide focused, hard light, floodlights provide diffused, soft light and are used primarily to reduce the wide contrast ratio provided by spotlights. Floodlights, which generally do not have lenses, come in five, sometimes overlapping, types: the *scoop*, the *broad*, the *floodlight bank*, the *fluorescent bank*, and the *strip light*.

The scoop is a half-melon, scooplike floodlight which is widely used and is now available in fixed-focus and modified-focus versions and in incandescent and quartz-bulb versions. The soft light the scoop provides can be made even more diffused by the addition of a spun glass scrim. The scrim not only diffuses the light but serves as a safety device should the bulb explode.

The broad is a rectangular structure usually using quartz lamps but sometimes equipped with fluorescent tubes; these tubes are not especially suitable to color TV production. Some broads have "barn doors" to restrict light and prevent its spilling over to areas where it is not needed or wanted. Some broads provide the opportunity to adjust the beam somewhat. Broads provide extremely diffuse, even light and some come with a permanently attached spun glass scrim and are sometimes called "softlights."

The floodlight bank offers a group of internal reflector lamps, usually in groups of three, which provides a soft, diffuse light through multi-source light overlapping but they are cumbersome and are less practical in the small/medium studio than they might be in outdoor lighting situations.

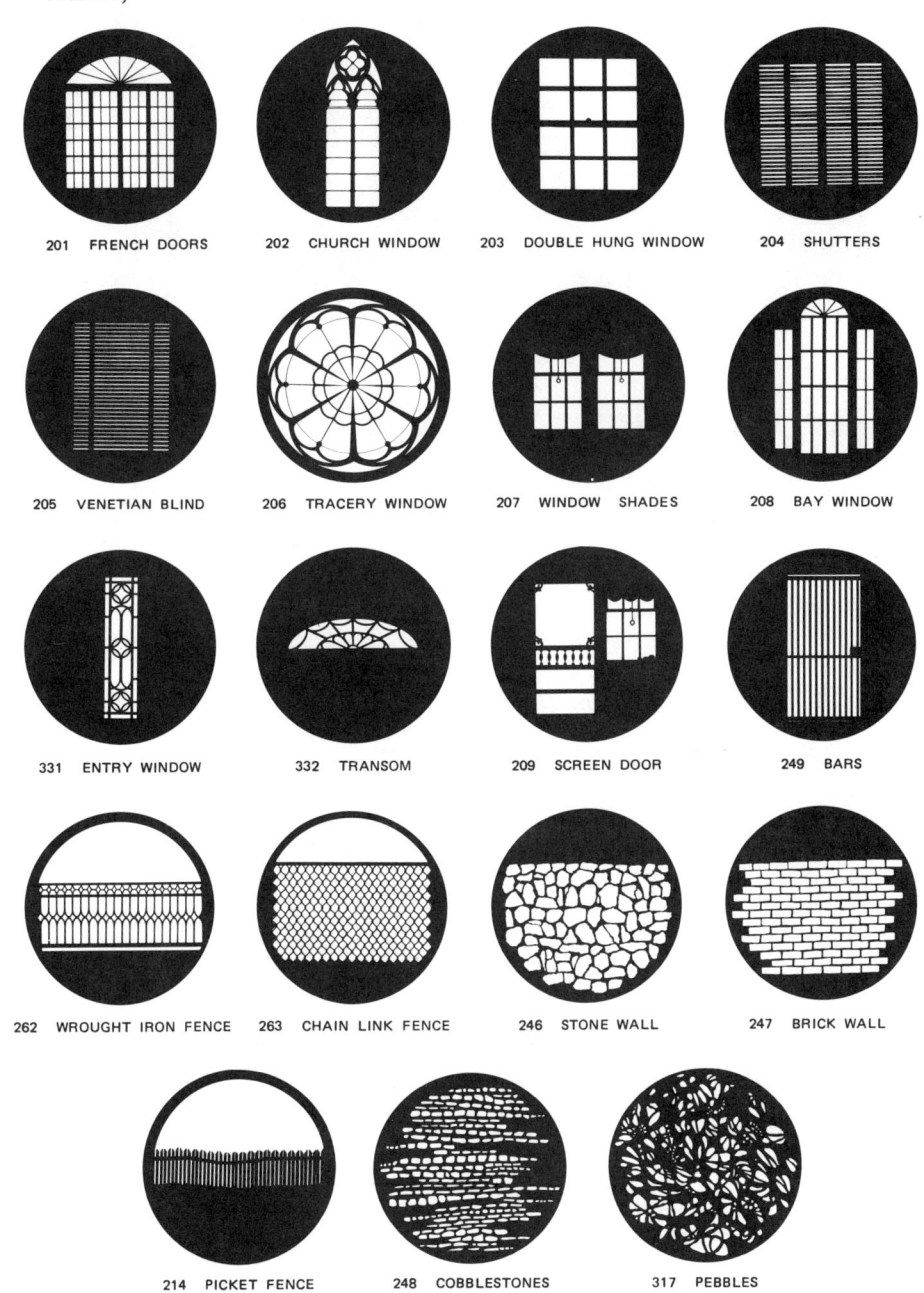

FIGURE 2-5a. Custom Cucalorous Patterns. (Courtesy of Great American Market.)

201 FRENCH DOORS	202 CHURCH WINDOW	203 DOUBLE HUNG WINDOW	204 SHUTTERS
205 VENETIAN BLIND	206 TRACERY WINDOW	207 WINDOW SHADES	208 BAY WINDOW
331 ENTRY WINDOW	332 TRANSOM	209 SCREEN DOOR	249 BARS
262 WROUGHT IRON FENCE	263 CHAIN LINK FENCE	246 STONE WALL	247 BRICK WALL
214 PICKET FENCE	248 COBBLESTONES	317 PEBBLES	

FIGURE 2-5b. Cucalorous Patterns. (Courtesy of Great American Market; lighting and photography by William Klages, custom pattern executed by Andrea Tawil.)

FIGURE 2-6. Scoop Light: Continuously variable focus from medium to wide flood. (Courtesy of Colortran, Inc.)

The fluorescent bank contains a group of fluorescent tubes which provide diffused lighting and is an economical source of light but suffers the disadvantages of being fragile and awkwardly large, or burning at a high color temperature, and occasionally causing interference with color camera operation.

The strip light consists of a series of small broads, or of internal

FIGURE 2-7. Broad Light: Has focus for beam control, uses Tungsten-Halogen lamps, shown here with *Barn Doors*. (Courtesy of Colortran, Inc.)

FIGURE 2-8. Softlight: Features high light output with soft shadows and four individually-switched lamps for intensity control. (Courtesy of Colortran, Inc.)

reflector lamps—usually from 3 to 12—connected in long strips. They are used to provide even, diffused light to a large, flat background, such as a cyclorama. Through the use of colored gels, they can provide appropriate colored light to the background.

Lighting Supports

In a small/medium TV studio, cluttered with crew, talent, sets, cameras and their cables, microphones and their cables, there is much justification for trying to avoid clutter when lighting instruments and their cables are added. Thus, studio lights should be located and secured overhead. The best way to secure lights is to install an overhead pipe grid to which lighting instruments can be attached. The pipe grid, consisting of pipes of about 2 inches in diameter, are hung as high as possible, in parallel fashion or crosswise, at least 2 feet below the ceiling and at least 12 feet above the floor. The lights are fixed to the bars by C-clamps or are attached to a moveable trolley to allow for horizontal movement of the light. Vertical movement can be accomplished by using vertically adjustable pantographs or telescopic hangars.

A more elaborate and costly system for securing lights overhead is through the use of counterweight battens which can be raised or

FIGURE 2-9. Cyclorama Strip Lights. (Courtesy of Colortran, Inc.)

lowered as needed and locked into place. The battens are arranged in a parallel pattern near the ceiling. Since they are counterbalanced by wall weights and operated by a rope-and-pulley system, the lighting instruments can be installed, maintained, and regulated from the studio floor.

Occasionally, suspended lights need to be supplemented by floor

FIGURE 2-10. Scooplight: On floor-stand, with spun-glass and chicken-wire scrim. Uses an incandescent lamp. (Photograph by Peter Dykstra.)

FIGURE 2-11. Overhead Pipe Grid. (Courtesy of Cablevision Systems Development Co.)

lights, especially when light is needed from a low angle. Usually, floor lights are mounted on telescopic roller-caster stands which can be adjusted vertically. Their main advantage is that floor lights provide precision lighting easily accessible to adjustment and that some versions of the floor light—such as the strip light, cyclorama light, and even spotlight—may be placed directly on the studio floor to provide light to areas of the set not easily reachable by overhead or otherwise elevated lights.

LIGHTING INSTRUMENT PLACEMENT

As indicated earlier in this section on lighting, one of the functions of proper lighting is to make three-dimensional objects look three-dimensional on the TV screen, which is actually two-dimensional in nature. Almost every chapter or article on lighting begins with a consideration of three point lighting—with good reason insofar as it is the system of light placement that gives dimension to the subject being lit and being "seen" and "shown" by the TV camera. The basic three point lighting principle is borrowed from the field of photography. It involves three major light sources: *key-light, fill-light,* and *back-light.* Respectfully, this book adds a fourth: *background-light.* Let us consider each of these three—or four—sources of light.

46 *The Lighting Person*

Key-light is the apparently predominant source of light among the four sources. It is a hard light (usually provided by a single fresnel spotlight) which, by casting pronounced shadows, shows the basic shape and surface texture of the object. The key-light usually is placed approximately 45 degrees above and approximately 45 degrees to either side of the camera lens axis.

Fill-light is a soft light (usually a scoop floodlight) whose purpose is to illuminate (not eliminate) shadows which may have been caused by the key-light. Fill-light is designed to augment and complement the key-light, not cancel its effect. The main function of fill-light is to reduce the contrast ratio of the picture, thereby enabling the TV camera to operate more efficiently. The fill-light usually is placed on the side of the camera opposite the key-light in a location analogous to that of the key-light: that is, approximately 45 degrees above and approximately 45 degrees to the side of the axis of the camera lens.

The back-light is a hard light (usually created by a fresnel spotlight) whose function it is to complete the impression of three-dimensionality suggested by the key-light. Its purpose is to prevent the object from seeming to blend into the background. It provides contour information about the object being lit. The back-light usually is placed directly behind the object being lit, again about 45 degrees above the axis of the camera lens. Much less of an angle might result in having the camera point directly into the back-light, thereby running the risk of damaging—perhaps irreparably—the camera tube. Much more of an angle might not only cause a distracting emphasis on the top of the subject's head (worse if he happens to be bald) but also might prevent

FIGURE 2-12. Key-Light only. (Courtesy of Cablevision Systems Development Co.)

FIGURE 2-13. Fill-Light only. (Courtesy of Cablevision Systems Development Co.)

the lamp from ventilating properly thereby causing the bulb or lens to shatter from the increased heat.

While the key-light, fill-light, and back-light work together to make the two-dimensional TV picture appear three-dimensional, it is possible that the resultant figure might seem suspended in limbo. To fix the dimensionality and placement of the subject, a fourth light source is needed: the background-light. In a sense, this changing of the three point lighting principle (the basic lighting triangle) to four point lighting principle (basic lighting quadrangle) would be achieved by providing an additional set of lights, separate from those involved in lighting the person; these added lights would be used to light the background. Usually, the background-light is a soft, even light provided by strip lights, consisting of quartz lights or internal reflector lamps placed right on the studio floor behind the set furniture; background-light may also be provided by a suspended multi-unit fixture. Should the direction of this background-light be discernible by the viewer, it should be consistent with that of the key-light to avoid confusion in the viewer's mind. Whether on the studio floor or suspended from above, these fixtures allow for the addition of colored gels as needed. The main function of the background-light is to give the three-dimensional subject some point of reference so the viewer will get some further idea of its shape, size, and location. The use of colored gels helps to accentuate the evaluation of shape, size, and location of the subject. It should be noted that the function of the separate background-light may be assumed by the key-light, fill-light, and base-light, should the combination of these three light sources be bright enough and evenly distributed enough and should the color of the background be suitable.

In addition to the four major types of light source—key, fill, back

FIGURE 2-14. Back-Light only. (Courtesy of Cablevision Systems Development Co.)

FIGURE 2-15. Key, Fill, and Back Light combined. (Courtesy of Cablevision Systems Development Co.)

FIGURE 2-16. Lighting Person, adding gel for background light. (Courtesy of Cablevision Systems Development Co.)

and background—a few additional, miscellaneous types might warrant mention here.

The *sidelight* is an optional light (usually a fresnel adjusted to the wide beam), which is located at a right angle to the camera lens axis. It is used to supplement the fill-light, to emphasize further the contours of the subject being lit. The *kicker-light* is a variety of back-light (usually a highly-focused fresnel spotlight) that strikes the subject from below eye level and from behind at an angle of about 35 degrees off the axis of the camera lens. The kicker-light is placed directly opposite the key-light

FIGURE 2-17. Sidelight only. (Courtesy of Cablevision Systems Development Co.)

FIGURE 2-18. Kicker-Light only. (Courtesy of Cablevision Systems Development Co.)

and supplements the contribution of the back-light to lend contour to the subject being lit. The *camera-light* is a low-powered mini spotlight usually attached right to the top of the camera. It is controlled by a small dimmer operated by the camera person. It is used to enhance and correct contours by reducing shadows, to provide localized light for title cards, and to highlight such facial features as the eyes.

Contrast Ratio of Lighting

Having considered the function and placement of such major light sources as key, fill, back, and background, as well as having mentioned briefly such miscellaneous light sources as the side, kicker, and camera, what should be the relative intensity—the contrast ratio—of the resultant light? Although such decisions by the lighting person would be conditioned by such factors as the mood of the program as well as the complexion, hair, and clothing color of the subject, and although in the final analysis how the picture looks on the monitor is what *really* matters, some basic principles of contrast ratio should be set forth. These principles should be known and considered by the lighting person even though they are subject to later adjustments and refinements as the lighting situation might demand. Generally, the lighting person might start with a key-light to fill-light ratio of 1 to 2 and a key-light to back-light ratio of 1 to 1.

LIGHTING CONTROL

How does the lighting person regulate the amount of light—whether it be hard light or soft light—that the camera "takes in"? Lighting control can be accomplished at the lighting instrument itself, at some control point elsewhere, and at the camera itself.

At the Instrument

The most immediate and obvious way to control the amount of light an instrument provides is to choose the appropriate type and wattage of the bulb. A second way to control the amount of light is to adjust spotlight focusing. As indicated earlier, when a Fresnel spotlight is spotted (or "pinned"), the lighting coverage is more localized and its intensity increases. When the Fresnel spotlight is flooded, the intensity decreases. A third method of controlling the amount of light is the use of one or more diffusers. Diffusers can take the form of spun-glass, wire mesh, or plastic scrims, which cut down and scatter the intensity of light that the lighting instrument gives off. Another type of device available blocks-off part of the light beam given off by the instrument, masking that part of the beam totally if the mask is opaque and partially if the mask is translucent. An example of the total masking variety would be the "barn-doors" that can be attached to spotlights or floodlights. Barn-doors are moveable flaps that can be moved into the path of the beam to reduce its height and/or width. *Flaps* are rectangular metal plates that block part of the beam and are attached to the instrument itself or are secured separately from the lighting instrument. *Snoots* are cylindrical tubes that are fastened to the front of the light and that restrict the spread of the light beam to a small circle. Another method of controlling the light at the lighting instrument itself is by making alterations in the distance between the light and its subject.

At the Lighting Board

Lighting can be controlled through the use of a dimmer board, usually located in the studio at some distance from the lights themselves or located in the control room. Essentially, the dimmer board regulates how much electrical current is permitted to flow to the lamp filament, thereby determining how intensely it will glow. Each dimmer is calibrated from 0 to 10, from no current (black) to full intensity. Each lighting instrument is plugged into a numbered outlet which is connected to the dimmer on the dimmer board (or "patch-bay") by a

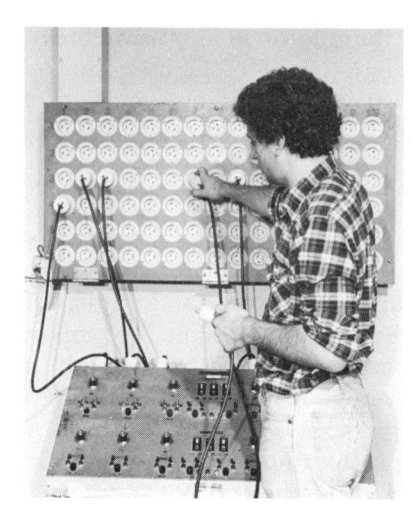

FIGURE 2-19. Dimmer Board below lighting board. (Photograph by Robert Lagarenne.)

numbered "patch." Several lighting instruments can be attached to the same patch and thereby controlled as a group, providing that overload is avoided. The dimmer board is a convenient device especially since lighting effects can be preset and recorded during rehearsal so that these lighting effects can be recreated quickly, efficiently, and consistently as needed.

Small/medium TV installations might be expected to have at least a simplified patch-bay and dimmer board, but even without these effective lighting can be accomplished by the other methods of light controlling described here. In fact, when using color equipment some small/medium TV studios prefer not to make extensive use of dimmers because when the electrical current sent to the lamp filament is reduced, the light gives off a reddish glow, thereby affecting the color temperature of the light being emitted. It should be noted that the adverse effects of this changing color temperature can be compensated for by using appropriate color filters over the light source. It should be emphasized, however, that dimming facilities are a "must" for achieving optimal technical and aesthetic results in more complicated programs.

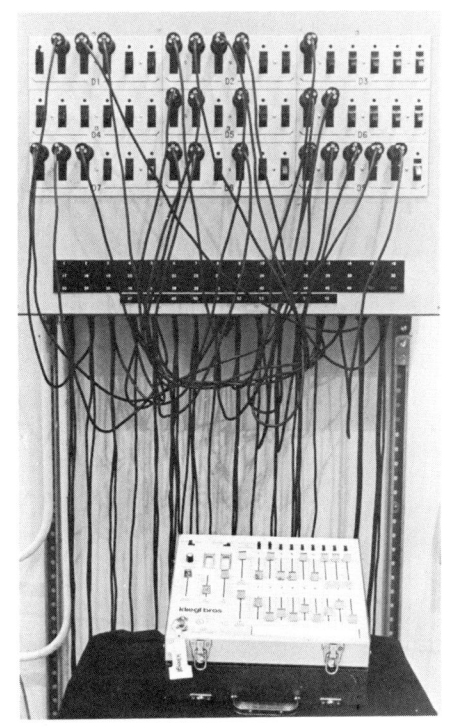

FIGURE 2-20. Lighting Patchboard with extra patches and portable dimmer board. (Courtesy of Cablevision Systems Development Co.)

At the Camera

Although consideration of lens aperture will be treated more fully in the chapter describing the camera, suffice it to say here that the overall image brightness can be controlled somewhat by "stopping down" the lens aperture (mindful of the negative impact this action has on depth-of-field, also to be described in a later section) or by placing a neutral density filter over the camera lens to allow less light to reach the camera tube inside the camera.

3
THE FLOOR PERSON

Essentially, the job of the floor person (sometimes called the *stage manager* or *floor manager*) is three-fold: (1) to do everything during the rehearsal and the actual production that the director would do were he or she in the studio instead of the control room (in other words, to act as the director's surrogate); (2) to do everything that needs to be done that no other crew person has done; (3) to serve as "live" liaison between the talent and the audience. Let us consider each of these three functions.

As Director's Surrogate

This section discusses only some of the ways the floor person can act in behalf of the director who is in the control room perhaps in another part of the building.

The floor person relays the director's cues clearly and calmly—but inaudibly—to the talent and sometimes to the rest of the crew in the studio during the program. These directions sometimes can be translated into standard hand signals. Some of the floor person's hand signals in general use are shown in Table 3-1. It should be noted that although the person demonstrating the arm and hand signals in the illustration here is not wearing a headset, the floor person does wear a headset which plugs into the intercom system in order to hear from the director the cues to be relayed visually to the talent.

Other hand signals may be created on the spot as needed. For example, such director's suggestions as "Smile!", "Sit Up!", "Put legs closer together!", "Stop wiggling your rotating chair!", "Stop drum-

TABLE 3–1. (See pp. 56–57)

Cue	Meaning	Hand and Arm Gesture
"Stand By!"	"Things are about to get underway. Get ready, get set—"	Floor person stands next to camera about to go on the air hand raised just above shoulder level, palm pointed toward talent, fingers pointing upward.
"Cue!"	"Go! You're on! Start!"	Points to performer.
"Speak Up!"	"Speak louder! Can't hear what you're saying!"	Cups right hand to right ear.
"Come Closer!"	"Move toward camera! Move downstage!"	Pulls open palms toward him/her.
"Move Back!"	"Back up! Move upstage!"	Pushes open palms away from him/her.
"Speed Up!"	"Talk or move faster—not much time left!"	Rotates hand and arm clockwise above head, speed of rotation dependent on urgency of the time situation.
"Stretch!"	"Slow down—too much time left—drag it out!"	Stretches imaginary rubber band between thumb and forefinger of each hand, distance between hands dependent on amount of time left to fill.
"Thirty Seconds Left!"	"Half a minute to go!"	Cross palms at right angles at shoulder height.
"Wrap up!"	"Wind up what you're doing—only 15 minutes are left!"	Rotates fist at shoulder level, inside of fist facing the talent.
"Cut!"	"Stop—show is over!"	Draws extended hands across throat simulating cutting action.

FIGURE 3-1a. "Stand By!"

FIGURE 3-1b. "Cue!"

FIGURE 3-1c. "Speak Up!"

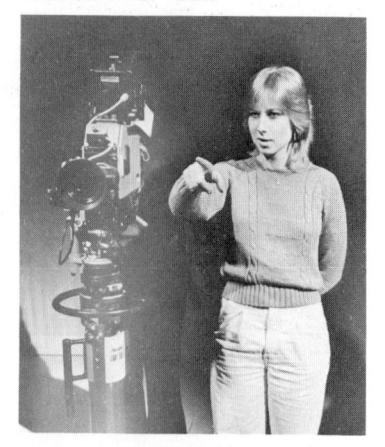

FIGURE 3-1d. "Come Closer!"

FIGURE 3-1e. "Move Back!"

FIGURE 3-1f. "Speed Up!"

FIGURE 3-1g. "Stretch!"

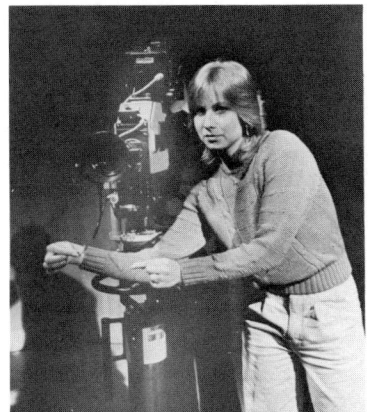

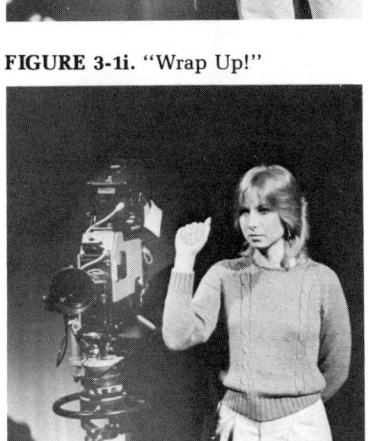

FIGURE 3-1h. "Thirty Seconds Left!"

FIGURE 3-1i. "Wrap Up!"

FIGURE 3-1j. "Cut!"

ming your fingers on the table, the mike is picking it up!", etc., can be communicated by appropriate pantomime and gestures by the floor person.

Sometimes the cues from the director are time cues in which case the floor person shows the talent the appropriate time card. When no time cards are available fingers are used to relay time cues. Of course, just before the program goes on and before the audio person opens the microphones, the floor person shouts out the time cues rather than using time cards, for the benefit of everyone in the studio, talent and crew.

Occasionally, the cues which the floor person must give the talent during the program are more extensive than can be communicated by a hand signal or a time card. Sometimes extensive cue cards are

FIGURE 3-2. Time Card. (Courtesy of Cablevision Systems Development Co.)

FIGURE 3-3. Cue Card. (Courtesy of Cablevision Systems Development Co.)

needed. The floor person should hold the cards so the line being read by the talent is as close to the "taking" lens as possible, so that the talent will seem to be looking into the lens, thereby minimizing the fact that he is reading. The floor person must be sure that when holding up the cue card his hands do not cover any of the printed material. Also, the floor person should not position himself behind the cards but should be in a position to read along silently with the talent in order to know when to change the cards. Among the problems encountered in using cue cards is that novice performers often have difficulty concealing the fact that they are reading. Squinting eyes, screwing up of the face, the sing-songey pattern many people employ when they read—all combine to make the performance stiff and unnatural. Also, cue cards must be hand-lettered, a process that is expensive in materials and man-hours. Using cue cards can be as laborious to the talent reading them and the floor person holding them and changing them as it was to the person hand-lettering them. In the small/medium TV studio cue cards are best used for those portions of the program that must be given verbatim—such as introductions and conclusions, for example—and for outlines containing main ideas, rather than used for verbatim transcripts.

Another prompting device that the floor person may encounter, especially in the large TV studio, is the *teleprompter*, a mechanism which enables the talent to seem to look directly into the lens as he or she reads a printed image on a glass screen positioned directly in front of the camera lens. The glass screen is located too near the lens to be

FIGURE 3-4a. Video Prompter camera attachment. (Courtesy of Q-TV.)

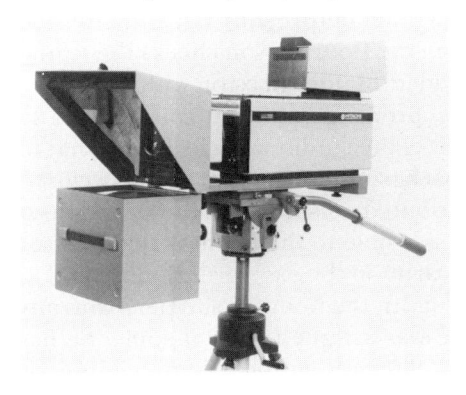

FIGURE 3-4b. Video Prompter script transport. (Courtesy of Q-TV.)

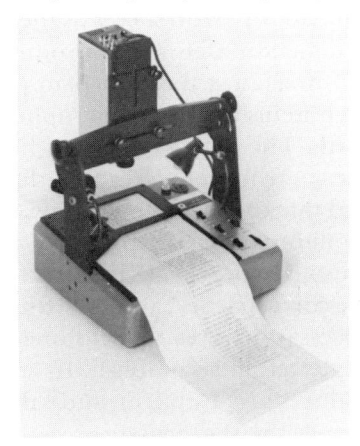

focused upon by it. The print is the result of a single-lens, closed-circuit TV camera scanning a moving script containing oversized print moving at a variable rate. The teleprompter is an expensive, cumbersome, and perhaps too exotic piece of equipment to be found in most small/medium TV installations and is mentioned here for informational purposes.

Whatever director's cues the floor person relays to talent should be easily visible. The talent most likely have bright studio lights hitting them directly in the eyes so the floor person should not be positioned in the shadowy darkness behind one of the cameras if he or she expects to be seen. The floor person generally is provided with a long enough cable for the headset; it should be long enough to reach any corner of the set. The floor person should move to the position which makes it most comfortable for the performers to see him or her without having to search—or even turn their head. All gestures—and all cue cards— the floor person wants the talent to see should be bold and clear and simple. The floor person should caution talent not to acknowledge any cues they have been given during the program.

The intercom connecting director and floor person is a two-way arrangement. That is, the floor person can talk to as well as hear from the director. Thus, from his/her vantage point in the studio the floor person can notice—or even anticipate—problems of which the director may not be aware; the floor person can relay this information to the director and then act upon the director's instructions.

As Studio Troubleshooter

The floor person serves as the crew chief before, during, and after the production. Before the production, the floor person checks the studio set-up against the floorplan provided by the director with regard to such items as lights, microphones, props, graphics, furniture, and so forth. The floor person synchronizes the studio wall clock with that in the control room, sees to it that background drapes are tightly closed and that the pleats are evenly distributed, ensures that the studio floor monitor is working properly and is visible to the talent if the director wants it to be, checks that the flip cards on the easel are all there and in the correct order, and so forth. In short, the floor person performs any necessary chores that no one else was assigned or that someone has neglected to accomplish. In addition to responsibilities to the director with regard to talent and "things," the floor person, as crew chief, supervises the activities of the studio crew, reminding the camera persons not to "burn in," not to stand on cables, not to behave improperly or unprofessionally or insensitively, etc.

As Contact with Talent

The floor person is the main human link the performer has with both the director and the audience. Talent, particularly inexperienced talent, need two things from the floor person before the program: practical information and psychological support, in order to cope with the alien territory that is the TV studio, with its lights, mysterious looking pieces of equipment, its earnest looking, intense crew and technicians who are too busy to offer much solace. The floor person should welcome the talent warmly and try to allay understandable fears. Since most fear is fear of the unknown, any quick orientation the floor person can provide the novice performer regarding the setting, the equipment, and the studio procedures would be appreciated by the talent. Would the performer like a glass of water? Where is the rest room? What is the reason for the apparently long delay? What are they thinking and saying behind that glass window? A reassuring remark—even a sincere compliment—given to the talent about how well he/she looks and how well he/she is doing would be most welcome and most appropriate. But inexperienced performers need more than encouragement—they need practical information about what is expected from them. What signals will they be getting from the floor person? Which camera will be "on" and should they look at it? How will they know how much time is left? Where are the props? When should they move, to where and how fast?

Two final points should be made with regard to the function of the floor person. First, his/her job is to execute the wishes of the director not to substitute his/her own. The floor person must exercise only as much initiative as the director would welcome. Secondly, the floor person sets the tone of the studio proceedings—by what he/she does and does not do, by what he/she says and does not say. Just like the director, the floor person should be as friendly as possible and as firm as necessary to insure that professional attitudes and orderly procedures will be observed by the rest of the crew and the talent in the studio.

FLOOR PERSON AND GRAPHICS

In the small/medium studio the floor person may have specific duties with regard to graphics. All TV programs employ *graphics,* which could be defined as two-dimensional visuals especially prepared or selected for use in a TV program to provide objective information to, and/or subjective responses in, the viewer. Objective information provided by graphics could include the name of the program, the director, the talent, the time and location of the scene, etc. Graphics which encourage subjective, emotional response in the viewer might include a photograph of a plane crash for shock value or, conversely, a photograph of a painting in an art gallery. Graphics may include printed material, charts, slides, maps, drawings, cartoons, and the like. Someone has to prepare or select the graphics and frequently in the small/medium studio that task falls to the floor person since the floor person, more than anyone else in the studio crew, is likely to be responsible for handling them during the program. Regardless of who actually prepares the graphics, the floor person might be expected to know something about them. Accordingly, this section sets forth some description, albeit a sketchy one, of what guiding principles apply to the design of graphics, what mechanical processes are available for making them, and what steps the floor person takes in placing and handling them in the studio.

Guiding Principles in Graphics Design

The first consideration in preparing or selecting graphics is that the information presented be oriented in a 3 to 4 ratio (called *aspect ratio*) in that the frame in which graphics are shown—the TV screen—is always in a 3 to 4 ratio. A picture of a giant sequoia tree would defy this principle. To capture the entire height the screen would have to include a good deal of the state of California or show blank areas on either side of the picture. Conversely, trying to get a picture of the entire kick chorus of the Radio City Rockettes would defy this aspect ratio guiding principle. To include the entire width of the kick line, the screen would have to show a good deal of the ceiling above the proscenium and several dozen rows of the orchestra. This is not to suggest that tall, thin pictures and short, wide graphics are totally useless. If the picture is large enough, the camera person might frame-up the bottom of the graphic and then tilt-up, thereby perhaps even embellishing the majestic height of the sequoia. Similarly, the camera person might frame-up on the beginning of the "kick chorus" and slowly Pan Right, thereby perhaps accentuating the number of dancers involved. (Incidentally, this is one reason why dance numbers on TV are usually choreographed in depth rather than laterally, from side-to-side.) It should be noted that while horizontally oriented slides match the shape of the TV screen, vertically oriented slides defy this aspect ratio principle and do not provide the camera person the remedy of tilting or panning the camera because slides must be screened full-frame.

A second guiding principle in preparing or selecting graphics takes into account the fact that there will very likely be a discrepancy between what the camera person sees on his/her viewfinder and what the viewer sees on the home TV screen. Since the TV viewer's screen *may* show less on the sides and/or the top and bottom, the graphics should make allowances for this possibility that some, or all, of the borders might be "cropped" after transmission because of the misalignment of the home receiver. Accordingly, in designing and framing the graphic, it is divided into three areas. First, the outer border (sometimes called the *dead area* or *bleed area*) is left free of information and is used for numbering, identification, and handling purposes and is not intended for inclusion in the camera's view. Secondly, the area within this border which the camera actually includes is called the *scanned area* (sometimes referred to as the *picture area* or *exposed area*). Thirdly, assuming that some of the picture might be cropped in transmission, a zone within the scanned area, called the *safe title area,* is used for the essential material to be transmitted. The area between the safe title area and the scanned area is called the *supplementary area* and provides the leeway for any picture loss. The safe title area is roughly 10 percent in from all sides of the scanned area frame. For example, the ubiquitous 11 × 14 title card might be designed as follows:

FIGURE 3-5. Graphic Cropping: 10% on each side of the graphic might be cropped in transmission. (Courtesy of Cablevision Systems Development Co.)

Many studios mark all camera viewfinders and studio monitors with a template or with magic marker outlines to remind camera persons and directors of that central area that comprises the safe title area lest some essential visual information be lost in transmission due to cropping.

A third guiding principle in preparing or selecting graphics—whether they are print, photographs, slides, or drawings—is that they be kept simple and legible and, in the case of print in particular, that it be kept brief. No more than six lines should be included on a graphics card. Two cards with three lines on each would be preferable. The print itself should be bold, solid, and clearly outlined. Fancy, scroll-like, finely-detailed print cannot be transmitted by the TV camera. (Incidentally, one way to tell, without placing the picture before the camera, whether the lines of a graphic are too fine for transmission is to squint at it through your eyelashes. If some of the lines disappear, they are too fine to be picked up and transmitted by the TV camera.)

As indicated earlier, sometimes graphics are intended to elicit in the viewer a subjective, emotional response. The "simplicity" guiding principle can be overdone in at least two situations. First, the design of the opening title graphic can help to provide a feeling, a "preview" of the material that is to follow. For example, if the program is to deal with a decorative, ornate, luxurious subject, a fancy background and not overly-stark print might be appropriate, providing neither damages legibility and providing they do not clash or distract. (Incidentally, such decorative backgrounds are easily available from decorators and from wallpaper stores, both of which have no need for "last year's line" which come in large swatch books; generally they will donate them freely and free.) Secondly, the urge for simplicity can be overdone when the logo of a product or corporation is involved. This writer was indelibly impressed with that fact when, as a fledgling TV director in the pre-videotape, "live" days of TV production, instead of using the official logos of department stores whose products were being displayed I used ordinary print! Thus,

Saks Fifth Avenue

Lord & Taylor

became Lord and Taylor and Saks Fifth Avenue. The design-conscious, traditional, almost sacred print logo was sacrificed in favor of practical, regular, objective print that, by comparison, had all the grandeur of a CARE package stencil! Needless to say, the phones began to ring off the wall not long after the program went on the air. The proper logos for these prestigious department stores were there for the next week's program but the sponsors were not!

Another guiding principle in graphics design is that contrast be kept in mind, whether you are using B&W or color equipment. B&W TV uses a gray scale, which is a chart showing the various gradations of the "color" gray that can be picked-up and distinguished by a TV camera. On one end of the scale is "TV White" (not quite pure white) and on the other end of the scale is "TV Black" (not quite jet black). In between are the eight gradations of gray. Although this 10-step gray scale is most frequently referred to in TV production literature, experience indicates that a 5-step gray scale is more realistic insofar as most TV sets can reproduce only about five shades of gray regardless of how many the camera can accommodate. Graphics are more legible, interesting, and attractive if they incorporate several shades of gray as well as TV White and TV Black. Contrast in color TV production (which will be covered in the section on color cameras) is determined by *hue* (the actual color), by *saturation* (the strength of the color), and by *brightness* (the darkness or lightness of the color). All these factors are to be considered—the over-riding element being the "taste" on the part of the person preparing the graphic to see to it that colors complement and contrast rather than clash. In designing graphics for color TV one should not lose sight of the fact that B&W cameras only differentiate the relative brightness of a color and ignore hue and saturation. Thus, two different colors with the same brightness will appear identical on the B&W TV receiver, thereby inviting contrast problems and, thereby, possibly causing legibility problems.

Graphics Production

Methods for making print graphics abound, ranging from freehand lettering to electronic character generators; the typical small/medium TV installation usually settles for something in-between. For example, Dry Transfer sheets containing rub-off letters that can be applied instantly are available from art supply stores. There are hot-press lettering devices in wide use that press heated letters into plastic film thereby "branding" the letters onto any background. A relatively new, though moderately expensive instrument and technique for instant lettering is coming into wide use. One of the versions is called the Kroy technique. A typedisc is turned to automatically position the desired letter and a button is pushed whereupon out comes type on a transparent tape which is then peeled from its backing and positioned on the graphics card. It is reputed to be 5 times faster than press-on lettering and twice as fast as mechanical lettering. Letter spacing is automatic and adjustable. Typediscs register 80 positions in 19 popular typestyles.

Should the small/medium studio equipment budget allow, print

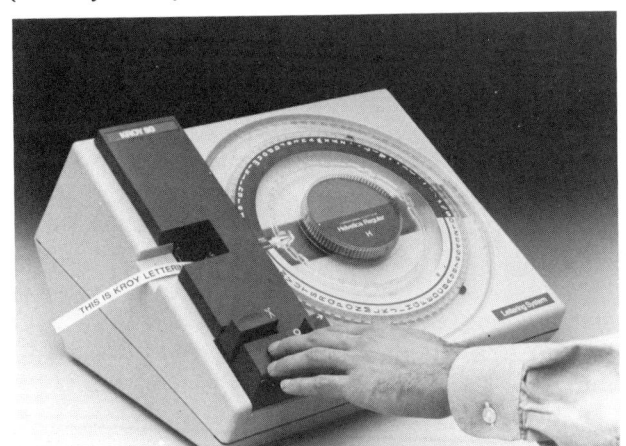

FIGURE 3-6a. Kroy Lettering positioning process.
(Courtesy of Kroy Inc.)

FIGURE 3-6b. Kroy Lettering peeling process. (Courtesy of Kroy Inc.)

FIGURE 3-6c. Kroy Lettering positioning process. (Courtesy of Kroy Inc.)

graphics can be created impressively and shown instantaneously by a special effects device that can generate electronic letters and numbers and other symbols. The character generator employs a standard typewriter/computer keyboard and can use a variety of print sizes and letter designs. The lettering is positioned on a monitor display screen by the use of a location indicator (a cursor). The print can be moved up or down, left or right, and can be made to roll vertically or crawl horizontally. The letters can be changed instantly and, through the use of a color synthesizer, can be printed in color. The material can be printed on the screen "live," during the program itself or it can be typed beforehand, stored on a floppy disc, retrieved when needed, and keyed into the program like any other electronic special effect (see the section on the switcher).

There are some advantages inherent in the time- and energy-consuming task of making individual letters and rubbing them on by hand that might compensate for sacrificing the speed and ease of having the print made by machine. Hand application permits you to space the letters *optically* rather than *mechanically,* thereby taking into account variations in the shape of particular letters, with more aesthetically pleasing and legible results, as illustrated in Figure 3-8.

FIGURE 3-7. Character Generator. (Courtesy of Cablevision Systems Development Co.)

Displaying and Handling Graphics

In addition to the electronic methods for displaying graphics just described, there are a number of basic, simple, and economical ways of injecting graphics into the program, including *easels, slides, crawls, front projection,* and *rear projection.*

With regard to easels, they may be of the caption stand variety (which have a tiltable, rotatable, liftable shelf), but a simple music stand, although less sturdy, is cheaper, more collapsible, lighter in weight and less bulky—all valuable features especially in the small/medium TV studio. One way to change print graphics is to have two such easels enabling the switcher to cut from one to the other, alternately removing the "used" graphic to reveal the next graphic on each easel. To save

LETTERING
LETTERING

FIGURE 3-8. Optical Spacing vs. Mechanical Spacing. (Drawing by Patricia Hopkins.)

67

room in the small studio and 'tie up one fewer cameras, all graphics can be placed on one easel. While still on camera, each of the "used" graphics are then pulled away to reveal the next, fresh graphic. The floor person must be sure to remove the card from the camera person's left to right so that the new print will appear from the viewer's left to his/her right, which is the direction in which we read in our culture. To have it go from right to left, against the grain, would be like rubbing the cat in the wrong direction! Pulling of the graphic card is facilitated by the use of card-tabs. Cards should be pulled as quickly as possible while still maintaining smoothness and a consistent rate. A blank, black card inserted between graphic cards can avoid the potential confusion of print immediately replacing print but sometimes a black, "no-picture" interval causes a discontinuity and a feeling that something is wrong with the receiver. If blank, black graphic cards are used they should be removed in the same manner as the printed graphic cards. A simpler way to remove print graphics is to punch holes into the border of the graphic card (outside the scanning area) and install them in a looseleaf folder so they can be flipped down to fall into the camera view.

In handling easel graphics in the studio the floor person should be on the alert for two problems: *keystoning* and *glare*. Keystoning takes its name from the shape of the keystone at the top of an arch, which holds the rest of the stones in place. Keystoning is an undesirable effect which is produced when the camera is not directly perpendicular, both in its vertical and horizontal axis, to the flat graphic it is "taking." The floor person should rotate the graphic clockwise or counterclockwise or tilt the graphic up or down to reduce the off-axis angle rather than call upon the camera person to make the correction. *Glare* can be

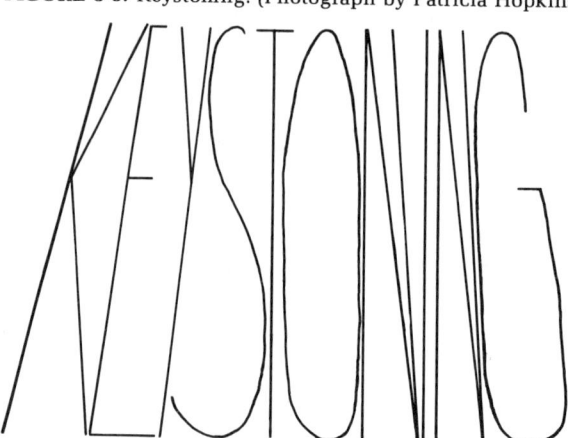

FIGURE 3-9. Keystoning. (Photograph by Patricia Hopkins.)

avoided by having the surface of the photograph developed in a matte finish rather than a glossy finish or by actually spraying the graphic with a commercial dulling spray which is removable, or with ordinary hair spray which may not be removable. The more immediate way to remove glare is to experiment with rotating the graphic at different angles from the offending light source.

With regard to slides, there is considerable advantage involved in having print and other graphics put on 2×2 slides, insofar as it eliminates devoting valuable studio space to easels and extra cameras. Even small/medium TV installations might be expected to have a slide projector serving its film chain in the telecine room. (The telecine room usually consists of a film island installation with a fixed TV camera

FIGURE 3-10a. Telecine Island. (Photograph by Robert Lagarenne.)

FIGURE 3-10b. Telecine Island. (Courtesy of Zei-Mark Corp.)

which picks up selectively the images projected into a mirror system by a slide projector and a film projector). If graphics are put on slides, they must be horizontally oriented in the proper 3 to 4 ratio, must be free of warping, and must have sufficient contrast. Incidentally, Polaroid is about to place a brand new device for preparing and mounting slides on the market. It should prove to be a boon to producing TV production graphics, particularly in the small or medium-sized TV production installation, which probably does not have a photographic lab on premises for processing film into slides. The device consists of a small unit about twice the size of a 35mm camera, making possible the immediate, on-the-spot developing and mounting of color or B&W slides from special Polaroid 35mm film. The roll of exposed film is fed into the unit and fused with a disposable roll of chemically-treated film as it is wound through the unit, emerging at the other end totally dry and ready to be trimmed and secured in cardboard slide holders. The cost of the unit is moderate and the cost of the disposable cartridge minimal. It eliminates the delay and bother of having to send the exposed film to a photographic lab and makes slides available almost immediately after the film has been exposed.

With regard to crawls, whenever the printed information to be shown is extensive, consideration should be given to using a crawl. The

FIGURE 3-11.

lines are printed individually and then attached to a roll of paper that is pulled from a supply drum to a take-up drum, much like rolling the film in a movie camera, although more slowly. The drum is rotated by hand or motor causing the lines to move up the screen since in our culture we read from top to bottom.

Front projection involves projecting a slide against a white screen in the studio and having the TV camera take a picture of it. The screen should be at some distance from the lights in the studio lest the spill from those lights wash out the image on the screen. This imposes some restriction on its use, especially in the small studio.

Rear projection which involves the camera's taking a picture of an image on a translucent screen projected by a slide projector *behind* the screen. This process "ties up" almost twice as much floorspace as front projection and therefore must be considered inappropriate for use in the small studio.

4
THE CAMERA PERSON

Essentially, the camera person's job is two-fold: first, to prepare during rehearsal the series of clearly focused, properly framed pictures the director instructs him or her to create; secondly, to make ready for use during the actual program these predetermined pictures before the director needs to call for them to be put on the air (or videotape). The picture designations (or shots) the camera person is called upon to provide may be classified according to *field of view, portion of the subject shown, number of subjects shown,* and by *camera angle.* It should be noted that all these classifications are relative rather than fixed and that all are subject to the interpretation and approval of the director. What a close-up consists of may be one person's opinion—but that "one person" is the director.

CAMERA SHOTS

Field of View

The first category of shots refers to the seeming distance of the subject from the camera (or viewer). The five major descriptions are these:

Extreme long shot (ELS) is a shot that gives an overall, broad, panoramic view; this is rarely used—usually limited to remote broadcasts to show outdoor settings or locale. Any people included in the viewing range of such a shot would probably be too small to discern or recognize.

Long shot (LS) would be of limited use in the small/medium studio

FIGURE 4-1. Extreme Long Shot (ELS). (Photograph by Peter Dykstra.)

FIGURE 4-2. Long Shot (LS). (Photograph by Peter Dykstra.)

except for possible use as an orientation or shot to cover broad movement on the set. The purpose of such an orientation or cover shot is to give the viewer an overall look at the premises in which subsequent, tighter shots will be inserted. It is to provide an informational, psychological, and aesthetic frame of reference for the closer views that will follow. When we enter an art gallery to see a mural, for example, we take in the entire frame before we focus in on any of the particulars.

The *medium shot (MS)* is the bread-and-butter, standard shot which concentrates on the subject and yet allows some view of what surrounds the subject, allowing ample room to gesture or change position if not to change location.

FIGURE 4-3. Medium Shot (MS). Photograph by Peter Dykstra.)

The *close-up (CU)* is particularly valuable in TV because the size of the screen is so limited, but it brings with it certain problems. The slightest movement by the talent—or by the camera—is exaggerated and can distract and annoy the viewer. Also, the depth of field of the lens used in the close-up is also quite limited. Finally, if the camera lens is permitted to get so physically close to the subject it might cast a distracting light shadow on the very subject it is taking and thereby include its own shadow in its own picture.

The *extreme close-up (ECU)* is just that: *extreme,* and therefore extremely rare. It has some legitimacy—as in science demonstrations when objects to be shown are extremely small, or in dramatic programs—but in the kind of program generally encountered in a small/medium TV installation its use is limited.

FIGURE 4-4. Close-Up (CU). (Photograph by Peter Dykstra.)

FIGURE 4-5. Extreme Close-Up (ECU). (Photograph by Peter Dykstra.)

Before leaving this treatment of field of vision as a classification of camera shots, two clarifications might be made. First, the word "long" in "long shot" means that the subject we are seeing seems like it is a long way off. This is not to be confused with the word "long" as it will be applied to lenses later in this chapter. Ironically—and perhaps confusingly—long shots are made by short lenses and close-ups are made by long lenses. Secondly, the word "long" means "long" only when compared to the other shots associated with it. A shot covering a boxing ring might be a long shot but if that same shot were shown in a shot context including the entire arena, the boxing ring shot would be considered a close-up shot.

Portion of Subject Shown

When the camera person has a person rather than a scene as the subject to be framed, the designation of shots can be less relative and subject to interpretation and more precise. To minimize confusion a series of designations has been developed which uses the lowest cut-off level of the human torso to be included in the frame as the identifying designation of the shot. Thus, a *full-shot (FS)* would be one that includes the entire body from toe to head. A *knee-shot (KS)* would be one that frames the figure from knee level upward. A *waist-shot (WS)* shows the figure from waist level upwards. A *bust-shot (BS)* begins at chest level. A *head-shot (HS)* begins at the chin level. Although these designations serve to describe the framing of the shot it does not follow that these shot framings are always appropriate. As will be discussed in this chapter under the framing section, some of these shots taken at natural cut-off points of the human body have aesthetic shortcomings.

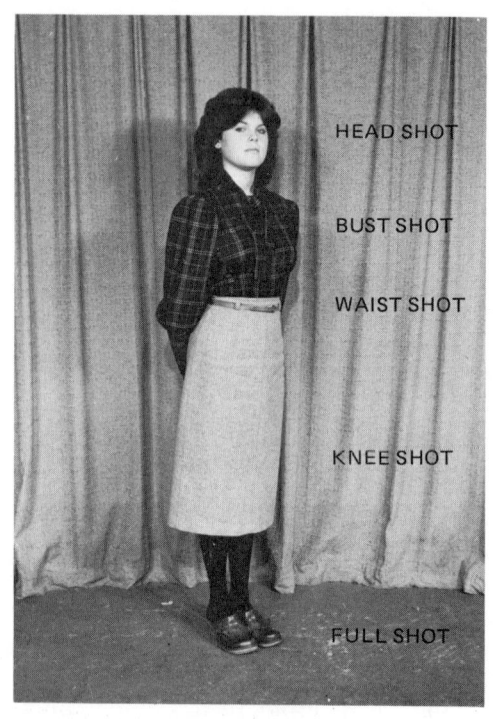

FIGURE 4-6. Framing Cut-Off Levels. (Photograph by Peter Dykstra.)

Number of Persons Shown

An even less ambiguous designation of a camera shot makes reference to the number of persons included in it. A *one-shot* is a picture of one person. A *two-shot* includes two people. A *three-shot* includes three people and a *four-shot* includes four people. More than four people becomes a *group shot*.

Camera Angle

The "normal" camera angle occurs when the lens is at the eye level of the subject being framed not the eye level of the camera person, the assumption being that if the subject is looking into the lens of the camera, he or she is looking the audience in the eye. If, however, the subject is seated or is lying down, eye level changes, the "normal" angle changes accordingly, and the camera level should be lowered. Similarly, if the subject is a child the grown-up angle would not be "normal." If the subject is a standing adult, the lens level for a "normal" angle

FIGURE 4-7. Normal Angle Shot. (Photograph by Peter Dykstra.)

FIGURE 4-8. Low-Angle Shot. (Photograph by Peter Dykstra.)

79

should be about 5 feet above the studio floor. When the pedestal is adjusted so the camera lens is several feet below this "normal" eye level or if the subject is raised several feet above this "normal" eye level so that the camera shoots up at a subject, the shot may be classified as a *low angle* shot. The low angle shot makes the subject seem impressive—even domineering. Dictators, like Hitler and Mussolini, recognized the psychological value of speaking from an elevated balcony. Children "look up" to their parents, both physically and psychologically (though, with better nutrition and changing social attitudes, this may be decreasing). Low angle shots must be executed with care and restraint lest the camera shoot off the set to show ceilings, lights, and the like. Conversely, when the camera lens is elevated relative to the subject, by raising the camera or lowering the subject, we have a *high angle* shot with just the opposite effect. The subject becomes something to "look down on." Many of the closing shots in the old Charlie Chaplin silent movies consisted of high angle shots—coupled with a zoomed out long shot—looking down on Charlie walking down a deserted street, making him look even more helpless and insignificant.

The *subjective angle* camera shot is one in which the camera becomes a participant in the proceedings rather than merely a spectator of them: the patient losing consciousness as the anesthesia is administered, seeing the operating room overhead lights spin around; the drink being lifted to the lips of the alcoholic; the blurry, bubbled vision

FIGURE 4-9. High-Angle Shot. (Photograph by Peter Dykstra.)

of the drowning man; the camera looking directly into the scientist's microscope. These are examples of the camera's seeming to become the person involved. The use of the subjective camera angle is not confined to dramatic programs. Instructional programs to develop motor skills and techniques—such as knitting, cooking, surgical dissection, carving—show how the process looks from the perspective and viewpoint of the person performing it so the learner will know how the process will look when he or she attempts to perform it.

Similar to the subjective angle shot are the *overhead angle* shot, the *over-the-shoulder angle* shot, and the *reverse angle* shot. As the name suggests, the overhead angle shot would be virtually perpendicular. In large studios with access to large cranes or a catwalk across the ceiling—or in outdoor sporting events like the Superbowl—it might be physically and financially feasible to position a TV camera directly overhead, but it would be impractical—if not impossible—for use in the small/medium studio. It is possible, however, to approximate an overhead angle shot by hanging a mirror above the subject and, with a little experimenting with angles, having the camera shoot up into the hanging mirror to "take" the image. The resulting image will be reversed. For those subjects with which such image reversal would distract and disorient the viewer, shooting into a second mirror facing, and parallel to, then should reverse the reversal and make things right. Apart from uses in dramatic programs, overhead angle shots are especially appropriate for such table top demonstrations as cooking, playing chess, and

FIGURE 4-10. Reverse Angle Shots. (Photograph by Peter Dykstra.)

82 *The Camera Person*

so forth. As the name implies, the over-the-shoulder shot involves taking a shot of the dominant person while continuing to show a portion of the person to whom he or she is speaking. Not only does this angle remind the viewer of the presence and physical relation of this second person but it also lends additional pictorial interest and welcome depth to the two-dimensional TV picture, rather than show the two figures in flat, "bookend" style. The reverse angle shot usually refers to a pair of matched over-the-shoulder shots.

Having considered the hardware of the camera, the physical act of getting a picture with the camera, what aesthetic considerations involve the camera person? One of these is pictorial composition.

PICTORIAL COMPOSITION

The director makes the decision about what elements are to be included in each picture assigned to the camera person. Once this decision is made, how does the camera person arrange these elements for maximum effect? This process is known as *pictorial composition,* which includes such factors as *framing, headroom,* and the *illusion of depth.* Not much space will be devoted here to considering these factors because they apply primarily to still pictures and good television is moving pictures; also, they are guidelines rather than rigid laws, often honored as much in their breach as in their observance. However, though not worthy of slavish observance they are worthy of mention and consideration.

Framing

Although the picture the camera person sees in the viewfinder is essentially the one which the director sees on the program monitor in the control room, if that particular picture is on the air, alignment might be off, with the result that some cropping (trimming of some or all edges of the picture) might occur in the videotaping process and/or in the transmission process and even more will probably occur in many of the home sets receiving the program. It has been estimated that from 10 percent–15 percent of the outer edges—top, bottom, and sides—of the original picture might be so cropped, making it a good idea for the camera person to frame the picture somewhat generously so that amount of potential picture loss can be afforded.

A principle frequently cited in writings about picture composition is the *rule of thirds*. Simply stated, this "rule" suggests that the screen mentally be divided horizontally and vertically by the camera person into three equal parts and that the camera person try to locate the major elements of interest in the subject at the four points at which the lines intersect. Unfortunately, most subjects do not fit so fortuitously into the mold and it might not be worth the time and effort to make them do so, especially since rehearsal time is usually at a premium in small/medium installations. Other suggestions regarding framing include that symmetrical balance of elements in a picture, the placing of the center of interest directly on the horizontal or the vertical axis, and the placing of the center of interest of a subject directly in the center of the frame are all examples of poor framing insofar as they are boring and lack pictorial interest.

Another framing consideration touched upon in writings on pictorial composition is the perceptual phenomenon known as psychological closure. This principle suggests that the human mind is capable of filling in missing parts of familiar objects in pictures that we see. For example, if *most* of a bullseye target is in the frame of a picture we can recognize what it is without having to see *all* of it. This ability to fill-in, to reconstruct in our mind's eye, serves the TV viewer well in that TV is primarily an intimate medium, making frequent use of close-ups, therefore of necessity cutting off parts of objects.

The psychological principle of closure, coupled with the admonition that some space ought to be provided around the subject by the camera person, give rise to another principle of framing, especially when framing the head of a person: either bring the subject well into the frame with adequate space around it or purposely leave part of it out of the frame to allow the phenomenon of psychological closure to take effect. If the chin rests on the bottom of the frame and the top of the head barely touches the top of the frame, an aesthetically awkward shot results—which might be labeled the "Signor Wences" effect, from the celebrated ventriloquist act that features a head in a box. The principle of psychological closure is not limited to heads. Bizarre—even ludicrous—impressions can inadvertently be created when the frame cuts the subject at one of the natural joints of the body. The camera person is well advised to cut the picture at some point between these torso or limb joints to prevent some of the distracting "amputee" shots that can result. Even when the full body is shown, ludicrous impressions may result when the figure seems to be resting, leaning, standing, or sitting on one of the edges of the frame. Again, the subject either should be pulled well into the frame or moved well out of the frame so psychological closure can come into play for the viewer.

Head Room

Head room refers to that area between the top of the subject's head and the "ceiling" of the frame. Aside from the already stated need to keep some space in framing a subject due to the possibility of cropping, there are aesthetic reasons why crowding the top of the frame can distract and detract. We are used to seeing some space around people; a lack of head room can make it appear that the subject is undergoing some discomfort and is trying to lift the ceiling with his head. On the other hand, too much head room can also distract, perhaps making it seem as if the subject is sinking into quicksand. How much head room should be provided by the camera person is an aesthetic judgment, not a mathematical one, but a reasonable rule of thumb is to allow enough head room so the eyes of the subject are just under ⅔ of the distance above the bottom of the frame.

While the term head room usually is associated with vertical framing considerations, there are some occasions when horizontal considerations apply to that same head. Often called nose room, talk

FIGURE 4-11a. Too Much Head Room. (Courtesy of Cablevision Systems Development Co.)

FIGURE 4-11b. Proper Head Room. (Courtesy of Cablevision Systems Development Co.)

FIGURE 4-11c. Too Little Head Room. (Courtesy of Cablevision Systems Development Co.)

FIGURE 4-12a. Dead-Center Framing. (Courtesy of Cablevision Systems Development Co.)

FIGURE 4-12b. Proper Lead Space. (Courtesy of Cablevision Systems Development Co.)

FIGURE 4-12c. Too Little Lead Space. (Courtesy of Cablevision Systems Development Co.)

space, or lead space, this framing consideration consists of leaving more space in front of the person's head than is left behind. Dead center framing, as was suggested earlier, lacks pictorial interest. Space in front makes a more comfortable picture and hints at where the person the subject is looking at is situated. Too much space behind causes the viewer to expect something to happen in that blank space—such as a pair of hands coming in to strangle the subject (perhaps a carryover from seeing horror movies). Of course, if a pair of hands is about to enter the picture to do the dastardly deed, the space behind would allow room and therefore would be appropriate. This principle of keeping "lead space" ahead of the subject applies to moving figures as well as to a person's head. Space in front should be provided in the frame to give the walking figure space to seem to enter.

Impression of Depth

To minimize the two-dimensional aspects of the TV screen, the camera person can sometimes make minor adjustments in camera angle and camera position to lend the impression of depth and of three-

85

FIGURE 4-13a. Too Little Lead Space. (Photograph by Peter Dykstra.)

FIGURE 4-13b. Proper Lead Space. (Photograph by Peter Dykstra.)

dimensionality. Subject to the approval of the director, the camera person might include an object in the foreground as a point of reference against which the viewer might judge the relative size and distance of objects in the middleground and background. A doorway or window, the corner of a chair or table, the shoulder of a person in the foreground beyond which the viewer sees the main scene—all these are ways to lend an illusion of depth to the scene.

Of course, the impression of depth can be fostered by the manner in which the director has staged the action, has arranged the furniture, and has chosen the colors to be used on the set and in the costumes. In blocking out the action, for example, the director would probably avoid lining up the performers in a straight line like so many birds on a telephone wire. Also, in a conversation, the director would avoid positioning them side-by-side like two bookends as was mentioned previously. Although it is not the prerogative of the camera person to determine the staging, small camera adjustments to accentuate the impression of depth might be welcomed by the director.

It should be emphasized that any effort to give the impression of depth—or indeed any other framing effort to achieve creative pictorial composition—that appears contrived or "cutesy" is best avoided. Like any creative effort, if technique shows through and becomes an end in itself, it is best to abandon it.

seems appropriate to begin the explanation of the camera head by considering the B&W camera head.

The Camera Lens. Whether B&W or color, all lenses have similar characteristics and functions. Let us consider, however briefly, the *fixed focal length single lens,* the *lens turret,* and the *zoom lens.*

The terms encountered most frequently in even the most cursory explanations of lenses are: *focus, focal length, f-stop, lens angle,* and *depth of field.*

Focus is achieved when the image appears most sharp and clear on the face of the camera tube and in the camera viewfinder.

Focal length of a lens, its most distinguishing feature, refers to the distance between the optical center of the lens and the face of the camera tube when the lens is focused at infinity. Fixed focus lenses are classified as *normal, short* (wide angle), and *long* (narrow angle). A normal lens has a focal length that corresponds most closely to the spatial relationships of normal human vision. What it "sees" is close to what a human might see from that distance and angle from the subject. A short (wide angle) lens allows you to see more items in the picture though they will seem further away. A long (narrow angle) lens will allow you to see fewer items in the picture but to see them closer up. For example, if the short lens allows you to see smaller images of several members of the choir, the long lens allows you to see fewer members of the choir but to see them closer up. In looking *at,* rather than through, a short and a long lens, we can distinguish between them at a glance. The short lens is short-looking, the long lens is long-looking.

The term *f-stop* refers to a number indicating how much light is permitted to pass through the lens on its way to the face of the camera tube. A glance into the fixed focus lens will reveal a diaphragm (or iris), the mechanism for controlling how much light will be allowed to pass through the lens apparatus. The diaphragm consists of a series of overlapping, flat metal blades or leaves. There is a ring on the lens barrel of a fixed focal length lens, which is used to open up or close down the opening between these leaves; this opening is called the aperture. On this ring on the barrel of the lens various numbers are etched—usually 1.4, 2.8, 4, 5.6, 8, 11, and 22; these numbers are called f-stops. The lower the f-stop number that lines up with the arrow on the barrel, the larger the aperture and therefore the more light allowed to pass through the lens aperture and therefore the more light allowed to pass through the lens apparatus. The higher the f-stop number that lines up with the arrow, the smaller the aperture and the less light allowed to pass through. If too much light is allowed to pass through *right!"* instructs the camera person to make the front of the camera move to the right. This is done by moving the panning handle to the camera person's left, causing the image to move to the left in the viewfinder. *"Tilt down!"* instructs the camera person to make the front of the camera move downward. This is done by lifting the panning handle, causing the image to rise in the viewfinder. *"Tilt up!"* instructs the camera person to make the front of his camera move upward. This is done by lowering the panning handle, causing the image to fall in the viewfinder. The adjustable friction controls (pan drag and tilt drag) should allow just enough drag or resistance so that the camera does not seem to "wobble," but not so much drag that it seems to "bite" as it is panned or tilted. The drag controls should not be used in place of the locking mechanism to secure the camera, lest the mechanism become stripped. Once the drag controls are properly loosened, the camera head allows more movements than the basic side-to-side and up-and-down movements. Circular, diagonal, and many other directions of camera movement are possible but rarely applicable to what is being shown.

In addition to pan and tilt, there are several other actions the camera person might be instructed to take by the director with regard to camera movement. *"Pedestal up!"* means to raise the level of the camera head, to increase its height above the studio floor. *"Pedestal down!"* means to lower the level of the camera head, to decrease its height above the studio floor. *"Dolly in!"* means to move the entire camera in toward the subject. *"Dolly out!"* means to pull the entire camera away from the subject. *"Truck right!"* means to move the entire camera to the camera person's right, parallel to the set. The term *"truck left!"* means to move the entire camera to the camera person's left.

Camera Head

The major components of the TV camera head are: the lens apparatus or external optical system; the internal lens and camera tube mechanism, which changes optical information into an electronic system; the viewfinder.

Although lower cost, smaller size, greater versatility, increasing simplicity of construction and the general appeal of color will someday make black-and-white TV cameras virtually obsolete even in small/medium installations, that day is not here yet. Many B&W camera chains are still in operation, especially in schools and other nonbroadcast operations. Adding to that, the fact that much that can be said about B&W camera chains is also applicable to color camera chains, it

FIGURE 4-19. Cam Head. (Courtesy of Listec.)

whether the base is a tripod or a pedestal. The purpose of the camera mounting head is to enable the camera to be rotated horizontally left and right and to be tilted up and down. The two types of camera mounting heads most likely to be encountered in a small/medium TV installation are the cradle head (see Figure 4-15) and the cam head. Both are designed to prevent the camera from becoming top heavy when it is tilted and both have locking mechanisms and drag controls to adjust the frictional resistance. Both the cradle head and the cam head operate on the principle of shifting the center of gravity of the camera to compensate for shifts in tilting angle. Both cradle and cam heads must be adapted to the particular camera in use since centers of gravity vary from one camera model to another.

Attached to the upper part of the camera mounting head is a detachable tubular handle of adjustable length and adjustable angle called the *panning handle* (see Figure 4-19). The panning handle is usually held by the camera person's hand, but it can be locked under the arm for more firm control; it is used to control camera head movement. The two basic movements that the camera mounting head enables the camera person to perform are the *pan* and the *tilt*. The pan (from the word panoramic) involves a lateral, horizontal movement from left to right or right to left. *"Pan left!"* instructs the camera person to move the front of the camera to the left, that is, the camera person's left. This is done by moving the panning handle to the camera person's right, causing the image to move to the right in the viewfinder. *"Pan installations, include its heaviness, which limits its portability, and its bulkiness and unwieldiness. Other TV camera bases, borrowed from film production, include the small and large cranes. Although they offer the epitome of flexibility, the demands they impose regarding studio width and studio height and the need for additional crew to operate them make them impractical for small/medium studios.

Camera Mounting Head

Continuing the description of each of the three elements of the TV camera, from the studio floor upward, we come to the camera mounting head, which joins the camera head itself to the camera base,

FIGURE 4-18. Camera Crane. (Courtesy of Listec.)

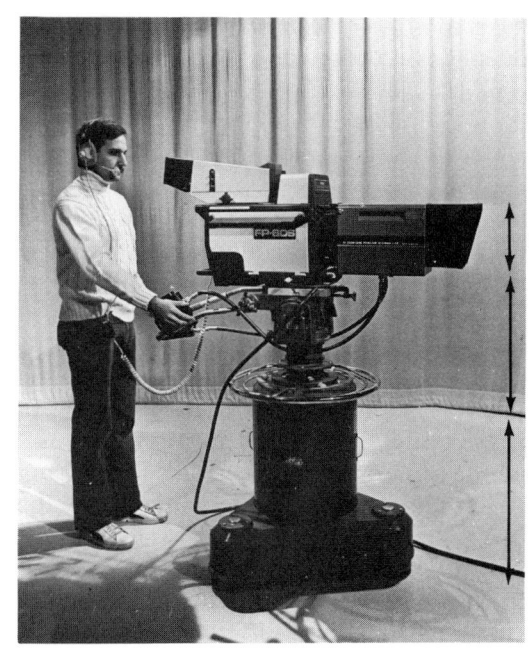

CAMERA HEAD

CAMERA MOUNTING

CAMERA BASE

FIGURE 4-16. Studio Pedestal. (Courtesy of Cablevision Systems Development Co.)

FIGURE 4-17. Pneumatic Pedestal. (Courtesy of Listec.)

90

lowering can be accomplished smoothly enough for on-the-air use, but at the very least it allows for quick and easy elevation between shots. The lightweight studio-field pedestal has extra large casters which can be locked in the brake position and set to move in a number of fixed directions, or it can be left unlocked to move about in a free-wheeling manner.

The *studio pedestal,* developed specifically for TV rather than borrowed from another medium, is probably the most widely used TV camera base—possibly due to its maneuverability, flexibility, and smoothness of operation. One of its distinctive features is a thick central shaft that can be raised and lowered smoothly enough to be done while on-the-air by a large ring; this ring is also used to steer the pedestal. Some of the simpler versions of the studio pedestal are hand-cranked. More expensive versions are pneumatically or hydraulically counterbalanced so that the camera person need only lift the ring gently to raise the camera. There is a second smaller ring to lock the column at the chosen height. Thus, one control handles camera height and camera movement simultaneously; both actions can be executed smoothly enough for on-the-air use. The main disadvantages of the studio pedestal, which diminish its suitability for small/medium TV

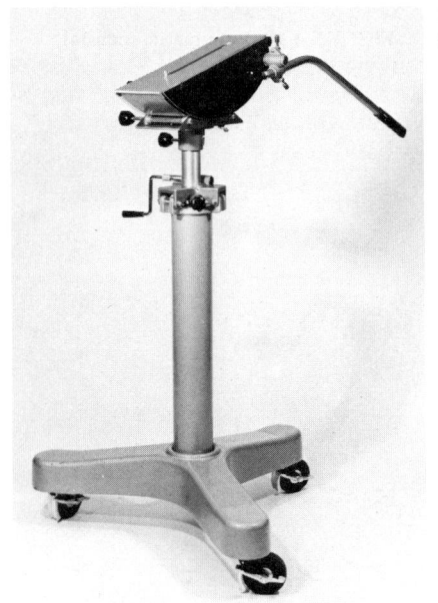

FIGURE 4-15. Studio/Field Pedestal. (Courtesy of Davis & Sanford Corp.)

the resulting picture will have too much contrast and too limited depth of field. Too little light will not provide a respectable picture.

Depth of field refers to the distance between the nearest point at which the subject is in sharp focus to the furthest point at which the subject is still in sharp focus without the camera person's having to make adjustments on the camera or having to move the camera. When the depth of field is considerable, the subject may move toward or away from the camera—or the camera may move toward or away from the subject—somewhat freely. If the depth of field is slight, the camera person will have to adjust focus frequently to avoid the subject's falling out of focus. Three factors which are interrelated and are not mutually exclusive in their operation are: *lens aperture, lens focal length,* and *distance* between camera and subject. With regard to lens aperture, the higher the f-stop the greater the depth of field. The problem is that lenses do not perform as well when set at lower f-stops and that with higher f-stops less light gets through the lens and therefore brighter light is needed in the studio. The heat and glare that results from such brighter light can exact a toll on the talent, crew, and equipment if sustained too long. With regard to focal length, the shorter the focal length the greater the depth of field. The problem the camera person encounters here is that the short, wide-angle lenses must work much closer to the subject thereby possibly getting into the view of other cameras, causing shadows that it or other cameras might pick up—unnerving novice talent, cluttering up the set, and so forth. If separating the camera from the subject seems like the most practical way to solve the problem of maintaining adequate depth of field it should be noted that small/medium studios do not allow very much separation and that such distance results in a smaller image—which might not be appropriate in every situation. Conversely, a lens with a long focal length offers more depth of field but might cause a problem for the camera person when trying to hold a shot steady—and even more trouble when dollying-in since the subject enlarged in the frame and the slightest movement is magnified. In summary, then, the camera person has to deal in trade-offs when dealing with the factors influencing depth of field.

Two points need to be made before leaving this cursory treatment of depth of field. First, there may be occasions when, for aesthetic reasons, the director might want to limit depth of field to keep the subject close up in sharp focus, but keep the background in less focus. Secondly, compensations for such potential problems as too much light can be made by adjustment achieved by the lighting control equipment in the control room and using neutral density filters on studio lights.

The Lens Turret. Having considered the fixed focus single lens, let us turn to a consideration of the *lens turret,* used primarily in B&W TV installations. A lens turret, located on the face of the camera, is simply a flat, round, rotating plate in which four sockets are located; as many as four fixed-focus lenses of differing lengths are screwed into these sockets. The sockets are located in the 3, 6, 9, and 12 o'clock positions of the round plate. Flat plugs are screwed into any unused socket if there are fewer than four lenses in use. As the circular plate containing the lenses is rotated either by a handgrip on the back of the camera or by a motor-driven, push button mechanism also at the back of the camera, one of the lenses is moved to a position directly in front of the camera tube and becomes the "taking" lens. Although the motor-driven change does take a bit longer to complete than the manual change, it automatically gets the pre-focussed lens thereby saving the camera person the time and effort to focus the new lens manually. Small indicator lights show the camera person which lens he or she has "racked up."

The fixed focus length lenses on the turret are arranged in progressive order from the shortest to the longest, usually from ½–4 inches in length, with the precaution that the longest lens not interfere with the field of view of the widest lens.

Were it not for the availability of the lens turret, the only way for a camera person to change a camera angle would be to unscrew one lens and screw in another, a time consuming, distracting, and awkward practice. The lens turret can be motor rotated in less than 3 seconds and even faster when manually operated. But even the lens turret has deficiencies. It can only bring the subject closer in a series of fixed, "giant" steps—and so the zoom lens was developed.

The Zoom Lens. Unlike the fixed focal length lenses described, the *zoom lens* is a variable focus lens—which simply means that instead of four fixed focal length as provided by the lenses in the turret, the zoom lens offers a continuous, variable focal length and thereby a continuously variable angle of view. The picture can be changed smoothly from a tight shot provided by the equivalent of a long lens giving the viewers a close-up picture to a wide shot provided by the equivalent of a short lens giving a "far away" shot. Not only does the zoom lens deliver the equivalent of the focal length offered by the four fixed lenses in the turret but it also provides an infinite number of focal lengths in between; the picture will remain in focus at any of these points within the zoom range. The zoom range, or zoom ratio, is the ratio of the longest to the shortest focal length and may vary from 3 to 1 to more than 40 to 1, the most practical for the small/medium studio being 10 to 1. Unlike with the lens turret, the changes can be made on-the-air without the need to cut to another camera, rack a lens, cut back to the new lens and, if the turret is manually operated, re-focus the new lens.

For flat subjects—like photographs, maps, and the like—the zoom effect is similar to dollying in with the camera. With three-dimensional subjects the only factor the zoom effect has in common with the dolly-in is that the subject gets larger in the frame. When the camera person chooses to dolly-in toward a subject the relative sizes of the objects in the scene will change proportionately and naturally. When the camera person zooms in the entire picture comes closer, but the perspective remains the same and the absence of any spatial displacement causes an artificial, unnatural effect. Zoom lens control devices range in complexity but have in common a mechanism for activating the variable focal length of the zoom lens and a mechanism for focusing the picture it takes. Some simple zoom lenses are activated by a little lever that rotates part of the lens apparatus clockwise or counterclockwise. Some more elaborate systems may employ a control rod that goes through the camera and emerges at the back where it is attached to a focus wheel. When the rod is pushed in the lens is zoomed in. When the rod is pulled out the lens is zoomed out. On some cameras the procedure works in reverse, pushing in the rod zooms the lens out and vice versa. The focus is executed by turning the focus wheel at the end of the rod. Some more expensive and complicated zoom mechanisms are controlled manually or controlled by an automatic "servo" mechanism in conjunction with the panning handle on the camera person's right. Similarly, focus control units are controlled manually or by an automatic servo mechanism, in conjunction with the panning handle on the camera person's left or connected to the side of a *shot box*. This shot box allows the camera person to pre-set a number of zoom positions and zoom speeds. Most small/medium TV installations are likely to have manually operated zoom mechanisms.

In order for the zoom lens to function properly to provide a focused image within its zoom range, the zoom lens must be properly pre-set, the procedure sometimes called "setting the tracking." With the B&W camera, the operator first zooms out to the widest angle and focuses the camera with the camera focus control. Essentially, the camera person is moving back the face of the camera pick-up tube from the lens. Next, the camera person zooms in all the way to the narrowest lens setting and focuses again, this time with the zoom lens focus control. When that dual procedure is completed the zoom lens is ready for use and should remain so unless the camera is moved to another location or the subject is moved considerably, in which case the tracking would have to be pre-set again.

With the color camera the pre-setting process is simpler, since there is no camera focus control in that camera pick-up tubes cannot be moved in relation to the front zoom lens. The zoom lens focus controls do the entire job of setting the tracking. The operator zooms all the way in to the narrowest lens setting and focuses with the zoom focus control and should be able to maintain focus even when he or she zooms all the way back to the widest setting.

Camera Tube. The major component within the camera housing is the camera tube. How much must the camera person know about the inner workings of the piece of equipment he operates? Probably not very much. How much must even Vladimir Horowitz have to know about the striking keys and felt pads inside his piano? Probably not very much. And probably the beginning piano student needs to know even less and the reader to whom this book is directed will probably never even lift the latches on a camera to look inside. One can enjoy a justifiable innocence about the innards of a camera, as with most other technical aspects of the electronic miracle that is television. While not knowing much about the camera tube is no shame, to paraphrase the "Fiddler on the Roof," it is no great honor, either. So, while a detailed, technical treatise on the camera tube workings is beyond the scope and intent of this book, at least a simplified, demystifying explanation of the general principles might be appropriate.

Up until the 1960s, the camera tube that was the workhorse of TV production was the image orthicon (IO) tube which provided excellent picture quality. The large tubes permitted the high resolution necessary to reproduce fine detail clearly and were free of the tendency to "smear" characteristic of other tubes. Shortcomings of the IO tube included its temperamentalness which required close (and expensive) engineering and technical attention, its need to be warmed up before use, its tendency to "burn in" if a picture, especially one with high contrast, were left on too long. The high initial cost and the high cost of operating and maintaining the IO camera made it necessary to develop a new type of camera tube. That new tube is the vidicon tube. Although the IO tube is still in operation, its shortcomings make it particularly impractical for use in small/medium TV installations, to which the book is addressed.

The major advantages of the vidicon tube over the IO tube include that it is cheaper and smaller, it is more rugged and does not demand expensive engineering pampering, it does not burn in as quickly, and it does not generate as much heat. These factors make the vidicon tube particularly suitable for use in B&W closed-circuit, educational uses despite its technical shortcomings. These include the fact that it operates at a higher light level, that its pictures are subject to "smear" more easily and that the pictures it produces lack the high level of resolution obtainable with the IO tube.

To understand the process by which the camera tube works, four principles need to be examined, three of these being electronic and the fourth physiological.

The three *electronic principles* involved in the operation of the camera tube are that light can be converted into electrons and electrons can be converted back to light; that a picture could be scanned to pick up minute bits of information and re-assembled on a plate; and that this video information could be modulated on a carrier wave for transmission.

The *physiological principle* is based on persistence of vision. The TV image is an optical illusion in much the same way that the film image is an optical illusion. Motion picture film consists of a number of still pictures shown in such rapid succession—24 frames per second—that looks to the viewer like a moving picture. TV depends on an analogous shortcoming in human vision. We see a complete 525-line image every 1/30th of a second, making a complete picture, known as a frame. The physiological phenomenon known as persistence of vision, which means the human eye holds an image for a split second after the image is removed, accounts for the fact that the individual frames seem to fuse together into motion. These electronic frames function like the optical frames in film to render the impression of motion.

Let us look at a schematic depiction of the technical process which incorporates these three electronic principles involved in creating, transmitting, and receiving the TV picture, to understand the role of the vidicon camera tube in this process.

The Black-and-White Camera Tube. If a TV camera is uncapped, turned on, and is pointed to even a minimally lit subject, the light reflected off the subject is focused by the lens onto the face of the vidicon pick-up tube in the camera. This photosensitive surface, composed of minute elements, is attached to a signal plate. As light strikes these minute

FIGURE 4-20. B&W Camera Picture. (Drawing by Patricia Hopkins.)

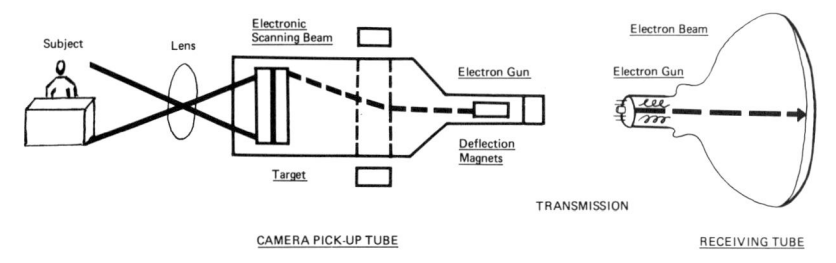

elements, photo electrons are released and picked up by a scanning beam projected from an electron gun at the rear of the tube. The electron gun scans the photosensitive surface very quickly, from left to right in alternate lines. The beam scans 525 lines across the tube front, 30 times per second. The odd numbered lines are "read" first in 1/60th of a second and then the even numbered lines also in 1/60th of a second. At the same time that the electron beam reads the pattern it discharges it. The disassembled original image comprises the video signal, which is processed and sent to an antenna, amplified, and transmitted in the form of radio waves. After these waves are picked up by the home antenna they are sent to an electron gun in the receiver tube; this gun is synchronized with the original electron gun in the camera tube. The electron gun in the receiver tube casts the reconstructed image onto a fluorescent screen which converts the photoelectrons into visible dots of light of varying brightness thereby providing a light and shade pattern comparable to the original picture, thereby re-assembling the original picture.

The Color Camera Tube. Most new color cameras use the *plumbicon* tube, which is a modified and improved vidicon tube. Whereas in the B&W camera the lens casts its focused image onto the face of the vidicon pick-up tube, the color camera by a series of mirrors and color-selective filters, splits the incoming white light into its three component primary colors: green, blue, and red. Each of these primary colors is sent to a separate pick-up tube. Thus, the color camera tube is really three separate camera tubes, the first to produce the green video signal, the second to produce the blue video signal, the third to produce the red video signal. Many of the modern color TV cameras contain a small, rugged beam-splitting prism block which simplifies and improves the light splitting process. It eliminates the need for internal lenses and mirrors and thereby the fragility of their delicate alignment. The three separate video signals are coded and transmitted.

The channels for these three primary colors are known as *chrominance* channels. In addition to color (or hue) there is the factor of brightness in the color signal. It is called the *luminance* channel and in the modern color TV camera is achieved by combining the three split primary colors back into white light. This luminance channel is particularly essential since the law demands that color cameras be able to convert the color signal into black and white images in order to accommodate black and white TV receivers. The luminance channel operates like the B&W camera tube described above. With regard to color TV receivers, the incoming signal is decoded to extract the luminance component of the signal for B&W sets and to enable each of the separate green, blue, and red components controlling its respective electron beam to function in the color receiver. Each of the three guns fires at the inside surface of the tube, which is covered with one million clusters of green, blue, and red dots, arranged in a triangle. A perforated mask situated between the guns and the coating of triangles enables each gun to enervate its appropriate color dot in the triangle and prevents one gun from hitting either of the two other primary color dots. The dots glow in proportion to the brightness of the original picture.

Camera Viewfinder. If an uncapped lens is lined-up with the camera tube, if the camera power is turned-on and if there is adequate light on the subject, the TV camera will "take" some sort of picture. Whatever that picture might be—useable on the air or not—it will appear on the viewfinder, which is usually located on top of the camera. The electronic viewfinder consists of a small, magnified picture tube that provides a picture of whatever the camera is "taking." Some viewfinders can be pointed upward or downward. Some viewfinders have instead a hood which can be tilted to shield the B&W picture from light spill; this spill would make it difficult for the camera person to focus the picture properly. The picture on the viewfinder must operate accurately and efficiently for the camera person to detect—and rectify—any deficiencies before the director needs to call for that picture to be put on the air or on the videotape.

There may be no electronic viewfinder on some simple cameras, in which case the camera person must pre-set the lens on instructions from the director or he or she must use a nearby studio monitor. Other simple cameras may have an open wire loop atop the camera to help the camera person estimate the area taken in by the lens. The only way the camera person would be able to do anything about focus would be to pre-set the lens.

Essentially, the camera viewfinder is a TV monitor and, as such,

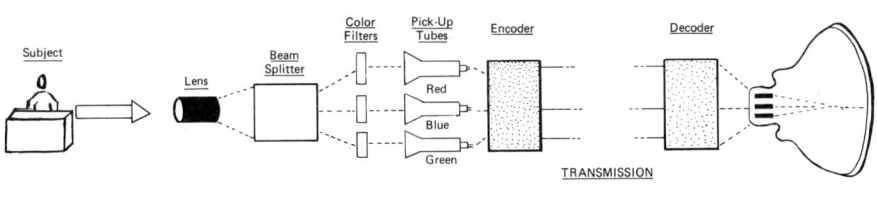

FIGURE 4-21. Color Camera Picture. (Drawing by Patricia Hopkins.)

has the usual TV monitor controls: brightness, contrast, horizontal hold, and vertical hold. These controls usually are found on the right side of the viewfinder (the camera person's right) and influence only the picture on the screen of the viewfinder and have no effect on the picture on any other monitor nor on the picture being taped or broadcast. These controls are used by the camera person to get the best picture on the viewfinder. These viewfinder controls should not be confused with those controls on the back of the camera that do affect the picture being "taken" by that camera and will be described in the following discussion.

In addition to features of the camera head described, the camera person needs to be familiar with a number of knobs, switches, lights, and sockets which appear on the camera even though he/she personally might not have to manipulate or otherwise deal directly with them. These most often include: knobs for controlling the electronic features of the picture; knobs for focusing the picture; switches; lights; sockets.

Most of the knobs affecting picture quality are adjusted only once, before the rehearsal or taping, or they are automatic, or they have counterparts on the camera control unit located elsewhere (usually in the control room) where they are adjusted by a trained technician with more electronic knowledge and skills than a camera person might be required—or expected—to possess.

The *vertical hold* knob, as the name suggests, controls vertical rolling of the picture and is usually set once before the rehearsal or the show and does not require much attention by the camera person.

The *horizontal hold* knob shifts the entire image to the right or the left within the viewfinder screen and it, too, is usually set once before the rehearsal or taping.

The *contrast control* knob controls the grayness of the picture on the viewfinder screen.

The *brightness control* knob controls the amount of whiteness in the picture.

The *target* knob controls the camera's sensitivity to light and it affects only the white values in the picture. The target knob has an automatic and a remote designation. Generally, the camera person leaves it on automatic so the camera makes its own light adjustments internally. If it is set at remote, the technician makes target adjustments at the camera control unit. In either case, the camera person has little contact with it once it has been set.

The *beam* knob also is set once by a technician and calls for no adjustment by the camera person. The beam knob is coordinated with the target knob to adjust the camera's sensitivity to light. A poor adjustment of these can not only cause "sticking" (a condition in which a moving figure will leave a sort of after-image briefly after it has moved) but might also damage the camera picture tube—further reasons for the camera person not to tamper with it. On some cameras the beam knob has two settings: remote and off. Remote permits adjustment of the beam at the camera control unit by a technician. Off is the setting for turning off the power to the camera.

In addition to the regular mechanisms for focusing described earlier, two focus knobs usually appear on the back of most B&W TV cameras: *mechanical* focus and *electrical* focus.

The mechanical focus knob is set by the technician beforehand and need not be touched by the camera person except as described earlier with regard to "setting the tracking" for the zoom lens. This knob brings the camera tube and lens closer together or moves them further apart, thereby changing the camera focus.

The electrical focus knob is seldom touched by the camera person except to make occasional, minor refinements, if necessary, after other focusing devices have been used to provide a sharp image.

Most cameras have two switches: *on/off* and *int/ext sync*. The on/off switch is self-explanatory but some have an intermediary station labeled *standby* which keeps the camera circuits ready so that the delay of having to warm them up is eliminated. The int/ext sync gives the camera person the choice between having the camera operate with internal sync or external sync. *Internal sync* enables the camera to provide its own sync to send directly to the videotape recorder or live audience. *External sync* is switched to by the camera person when several cameras are in use so that cameras, monitors, and videotape recorder circuits are synchonized.

Most B&W cameras have a set of tally lights. A small, red tally light is located next to the viewfinder screen. When it glows the camera person knows that the camera is taking the picture that is on-the-air (or on the videotape). When it goes off, the camera person knows that some other camera's picture is "on" and that, therefore, he/she is free to get the next shot ready. Analogous to this small tally light on the back of the camera is a much larger one on the front of the camera so the talent and floor person will know which camera is "on." This larger tally light usually shows by means of a large black number affixed to it the number of the camera.

With regard to sockets, most B&W cameras have two sockets into which a jack (or plug) at the end of a headset can be plugged. Into one of these is plugged the camera person's headset; if the floor person does not have a headset and long cable plugged into a separate wall socket, the floor person's headset is plugged into the second socket on the camera. All studio crew and control room production personnel wearing a headset plugged into the intercom system can talk to or hear from anyone else wearing such a headset. Usually the flow of communication is from the director to the studio crew, especially during the actual program as opposed to during the rehearsal. Should the camera person, however, have to ask or tell the director something during the program, he/she cups a hand over the mouthpiece of the headset, turns away from the talent's microphones (lest they pick-up and "broadcast" these remarks), and speaks in a hushed tone.

5 THE SWITCHER

In the early days of TV production, the director was not permitted to talk through the intercom directly to the camera persons—known as camera*men* in those days. The director had to address instructions to the *technical director (TD)*, who in turn would relay the order to the crew in the studio. The TD was then a supervisor of all the production crew personnel, including camera persons. The time lag involved in the director's calling for a camera movement, the TD's comprehending it and relaying it to the camera person, and the camera person's comprehending it and executing it caused that system to be abandoned eventually.

The system now most widely in use allows the director to talk directly to the entire crew including the TD—whose job it is now to operate the switching system. In some small studios the director does his/her own switching. This has the advantage of eliminating one step—that of having the director relay decisions through another person, the TD—but it does add one more chore for the already burdened director.

The switcher's job—whoever executes it—is to switch the picture the audience sees—or the videotape records—from the picture one camera shows to the picture another camera shows. A complex switching board can look quite forbidding—even frightening. Fortunately, it is not as difficult to operate as it might seem at first glance. For simplicity's sake, let us divide our consideration of the switching operation into two categories: *reality* switching and *special effects* switching.

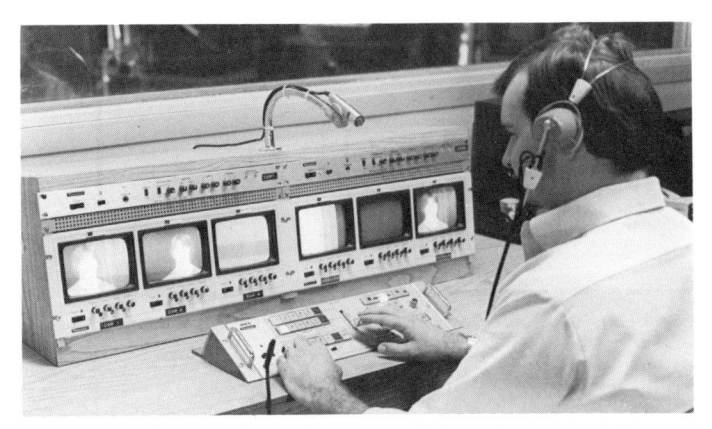

FIGURE 5-1. Director doing his own switching. (Photograph by Francis De Petris.)

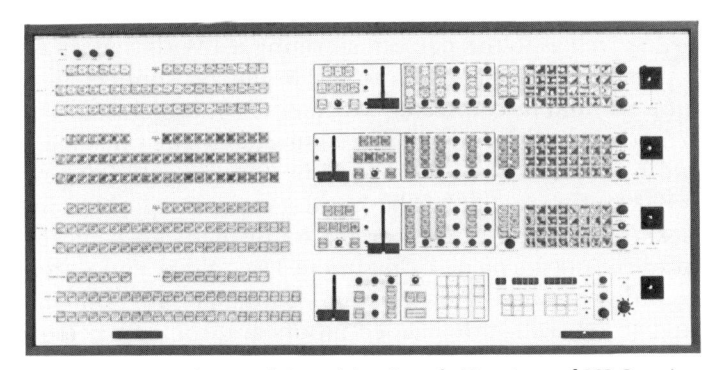

FIGURE 5-2. Professional Switching Board. (Courtesy of ISI Corp.)

REALITY SWITCHES

It should be noted that approximately 90 percent of the switches (transitions) from one camera to another called for by the director and executed by the switcher are reality switches. All "reality" programs—news, interviews, panel discussions, cooking shows, quiz shows—which aim to show something actually happening, without production-technique embellishment, use the switching process known as a *cut*. The definition of a cut is a switch from one camera's picture (or from black, or no picture) to another camera's picture (or to black) *instantaneously*. The change is accomplished literally with split-second speed.

Theoretically, if all we ever wanted to do was to switch from one camera's picture to another camera's picture instantaneously all we

107

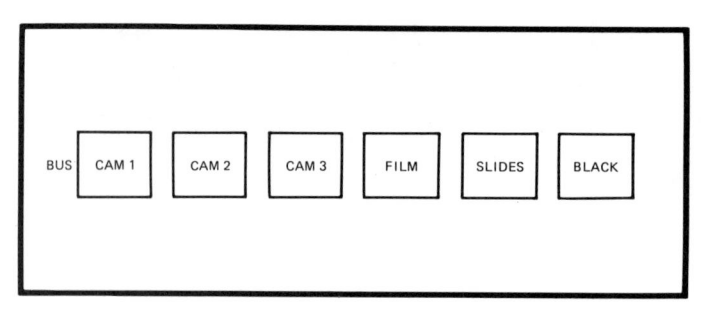

FIGURE 5-3. One-Bus Switching. (Drawing by Patricia Hopkins.)

would need is one row of buttons (called a "bus"), with one button for each camera (or other video source) and with each input wired to the switcher and one button for black. The switcher would serve as a sort of basic connection box. (Incidentally, the word "switcher" refers to the switching board as well as to the person operating it.) With that primitive but functional arrangement, button 1 would be connected to camera 1, button 2 would be connected to camera 2, button 3 would be connected to camera 3, button 4 would be connected to the film chain, button 5 would be connected to slides, and button 6 would have no video input and therefore would be blank and serve as the position for cutting to black. Thus, if button 1 were to be pushed down by the switcher, its video input (the picture on camera 1) would be connected to the video output cable and thus go on-the-air (or on the videotape)—and so on, with other video inputs and their respective buttons. As soon as the particular button is depressed, that camera's picture pops up on the program monitor instantaneously.

If all we wanted to do in a program was show one picture after

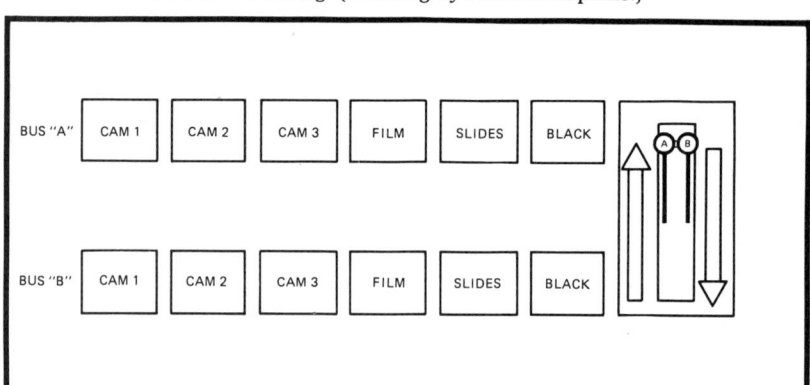

FIGURE 5-4. Two-Bus Switching. (Drawing by Patricia Hopkins.)

108

another, all we would need would be such a row of six buttons (a bus). But cuts account for only 90 percent of the switches; the remaining 10 percent of the switches involve effects other than the cut. To avoid the monotony and aesthetic limitation of having only cuts available for switching, most switchers have at least one additional row of buttons (a bus) and a pair of levers (an A bus lever and a B bus lever), that usually operate jointly but which can be made to operate independently. This second row of buttons (bus B) and the two levers enable the switcher to do more than cut instantaneously from one camera's picture to another's. They enable him to execute switches that comprise the remaining 10 percent of switching transitions: the *fade,* the *dissolve,* and the *super.* These three comprise "special effects" switching and are employed in such other than "reality" programs as drama, dance, music, and other such "illusion" programs.

SPECIAL EFFECTS SWITCHES

To understand how special effects switches are accomplished, we must take a good look at the action of the levers mentioned above. For the time being let us consider these two levers as one lever, even though under special circumstances to be described later they can be made to function independently of each other.

One basic principle involved in switching must be made clear at the very outset: with one exception to be described later, only one of the two rows of buttons can be "live" at any given time. If we have two busses, bus A and bus B, and two levers, Lever A and Lever B operating as one lever, when the switcher lifts the lever to bus A that bus is working and the other, bus B, is idle. Conversely, when the switcher lowers the lever to bus B, that bus is live and the other, bus A, is dead. In other words, the row of buttons at which the "lever" is located is the live row and will respond to the buttons being depressed by the switcher.

Having established that principle, let us consider how the three special effects switches—the fade, the dissolve, and the super—are defined and how they can be achieved by the switcher.

The Fade

A fade-in is a gradual transition from no picture (black) to a picture. A fade-out is a gradual transition from a picture to no picture (black). Assuming that button 6 (the button for blank since there is no video input connected to it) is depressed, the director might call for a fade-in of camera 1's picture, by saying "Ready to fade-in 1!" The switcher would check to see which bus the lever is on. The switcher would not push down button 1 on that bus because that would cut to camera 1's picture, putting it on the air instantaneously and the director wants to fade it in gradually. Instead of depressing button 1 on the bus with the levers, the switcher depresses button 1 on the idle, dead bus. When the switcher depresses that button nothing happens yet. The switcher has merely alerted that button for imminent use. When the director orders "Fade-in 1!", the switcher gradually moves the lever to the row of buttons on which camera 1's button was depressed, thereby gradually activating that row and bringing in that camera's picture. The switcher continues to use that particular row of buttons now that it is live for all subsequent cuts to be ordered by the director. The switcher thinks in terms of the opposite idle bus only should the director call for one of the three special effects: the fade, the dissolve, or the super. For example, when the director orders "Ready to fade-out!", the switcher pushes down button 6 (for which there is no video source and is therefore blank, used for black) on the row of buttons opposite the levers. Again, nothing happens because that row of buttons does not have the "lever" and is therefore dead. When the director orders "Fade-out!" the switcher gradually moves the "lever" to that bus and the picture on-the-air gradually goes to black.

The Dissolve

A dissolve is like a cut insofar as the switch is from one camera's picture to another's, except that instead of the switch being done instantaneously it is done gradually. A dissolve is also like a fade-in insofar as to execute it the switcher on the "Ready" cue from the director depresses the desired button on the bus on which the lever is *not* located in order to alert that bus for imminent use. The dissolve actually takes place on the director's command "Dissolve to _____!", at which point the switcher gradually moves the lever toward the newly depressed button.

The Super

When using a still camera, if the operator forgets to advance the roll of film to the next number on the roll, a double exposure results and the picture that results is ruined. A *super* in TV switching is an *intentional* double exposure. The pictures from two separate cameras are presented on the air simultaneously. For example, if a vocalist is performing in front of a black background, camera 1 might show only the face of the vocalist in the lower left part of its frame and camera 2 might show the entire torso in the upper right corner of its frame. Since black does not "photograph" in TV, when both these shots are shown simultaneously on the program monitor only the two differing views of the performer appear, making a creative picture suited to the subject matter. Similarly, in another sequence, camera 1 might show a newscaster about to begin reading and camera 2 might show a graphic in which white letters against a black background spelled out the name of the show or the newscaster. When camera 1's and camera 2's picture are put on the air simultaneously, we see the newscaster at his desk and "supered" over his image the white letters on the graphic since, again, black does not "photograph" in TV. In a sense, a super is a dissolve frozen in place. The super is achieved by the switcher by placing the lever approximately midway between the rows of buttons. Should the switcher want to make one of the pictures stronger (such as making the white print appear whiter, for example), he/she can "cheat" a bit by nudging the lever a bit more toward the depressed button of the image he/she wants to strengthen.

Up to this point we have suggested that the A bus lever and the B bus lever be kept together and considered to be one lever. What is the significance and advantage of having these separate? One situation in which their separation might be advantageous would be when the switcher wants to fade from a super to black. Both levers would be approximately midway between the busses. By lowering the A bus lever to the B bus and simultaneously raising the B bus lever to the A bus, both pictures would fade out.

Another occasion in which separating the handles might be needed would be if the switcher were called upon by the director, for artistic and creative reasons, to provide a *cross-fade*. A cross-fade in TV

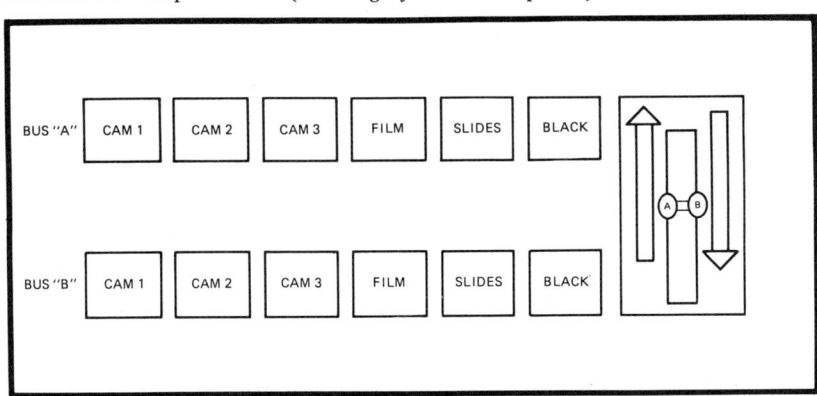

FIGURE 5-5. "Super" Effect. (Drawing by Patricia Hopkins.)

is analogous to a cross-fade in audio except that it uses picture rather than sound. A TV cross-fade is an interrupted dissolve, in which a period of blackness, or no picture, might be desired between one picture melting away and the next picture's being brought in. To accomplish this effect the switcher simply separates the levers as he/she moves the relevant lever (the B bus lever if the levers were on the B bus and the A bus lever if the levers were on the A bus) from the bus that is on the air to remove that image and then, after an interval, moves the remaining lever to join the other one. A cross-fade is a split dissolve.

MORE ADVANCED SWITCHERS

By way of simplification—and to counteract the formidable, somewhat awesome impression the switching unit makes—we have considered two somewhat primitive switching apparatuses: the one-bus and the two-bus switchers. We come now to a consideration of the slightly more complicated switching apparatus probably most widely used in small/medium installations: the four-bus switcher.

The four-bus switcher adds two busses to the A bus and the B bus just described: the *program bus* and the *preview bus*.

The Program Bus

Essentially, the program bus duplicates much of the function of the two-bus switchers but it adds considerable versatility to the switcher.

FIGURE 5-6. Four-Bus Switcher. (Drawing by Patricia Hopkins.)

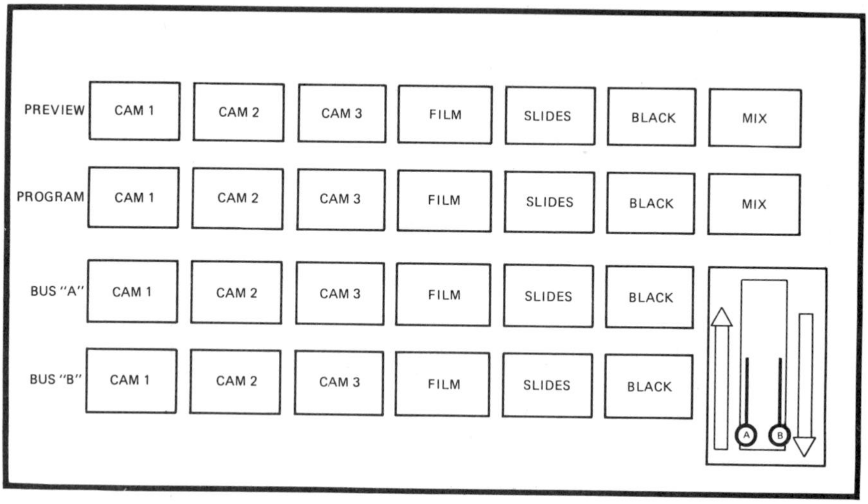

PREVIEW	CAM 1	CAM 2	CAM 3	FILM	SLIDES	BLACK	MIX
PROGRAM	CAM 1	CAM 2	CAM 3	FILM	SLIDES	BLACK	MIX
BUS "A"	CAM 1	CAM 2	CAM 3	FILM	SLIDES	BLACK	
BUS "B"	CAM 1	CAM 2	CAM 3	FILM	SLIDES	BLACK	

The program bus is a direct input-output link, much like the one-bus described earlier so that any button depressed on that bus pops right up on the air. Its most important button is the mix button. When the mix button has been depressed whatever is punched up on the A bus and/or the B bus is on-the-air. Most of the time the switcher would use the mix busses for cuts, dissolves, fades, and supers with the mix bus on the program bus depressed. The program bus allows the switcher to punch up directly any video source he/she chooses, thereby freeing the mix busses and levers for other purposes.

The Preview Bus

A second row of buttons—the *preview bus*—is added to the two-bus switcher described earlier. It is very similar to the program bus except that, as the name suggests, it permits what is to be seen to appear on a special preview monitor rather than on the on-the-air program line. The director is thereby able to preview an individual picture—or to pre-set a special effect—and check it before it goes out on-the-air or on the videotape recording.

ELECTRONIC SPECIAL EFFECTS

In addition to the previously mentioned special effects—the fade, the dissolve, and the super—there are a number of "special" special effects that can be executed should the switcher apparatus come equipped with a special effects generator, as most of them do these days. An additional row of buttons and a second set of fading levers are provided. These effects are known as "electronic" effects, somewhat of a misnomer insofar as all the other effects the switching mechanism makes are also electronically achieved. (In fact, the entire TV studio is

FIGURE 5-7. Small Special Effects Generator.
(Photograph by Francis De Petris.)

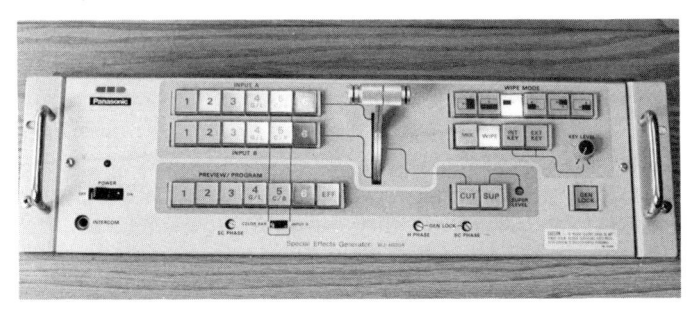

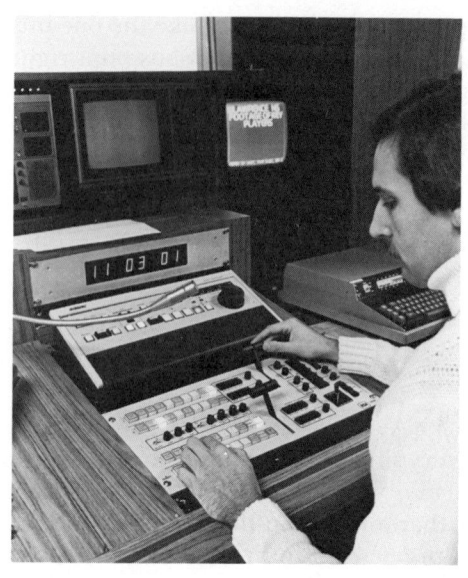

FIGURE 5-8. Medium-Size Switcher. (Courtesy of Cablevision Systems Development Co.)

electronically operated.) These effects will not be described extensively here not only because some switchers used in small/medium TV stations do not have special effects generators but also because these effects are a bit gimmicky and cutesy—and perhaps a bit ostentatious and too exotic for the practical, utilitarian programs which the small/medium installations encounter. Since special electronic effects, if properly employed, can enhance a TV program some brief consideration of what they are and how they are achieved is included here. The electronic effects to be described here include the *key,* the *matte,* the *chroma-key,* the *wipe,* and the *split screen.*

The Key

In our consideration of the "regular" special effects which collectively comprise 10 percent of the switches made, mention was made of the super. It was accomplished by placing the lever approximately midway between the two busses. Half the signal strength from each of the video sources connected to the buttons that were depressed were combined for the double exposure effect that resulted. One of the examples of its use that was cited described white letters superimposed over the image of a newscaster. The problem here is that since both pictures are at half strength a murky picture sometimes results and also the white letters might not be white enough, thereby allowing some of the background detail to "show through" the white lettering. The internal *key* mode on the special effects generator allows the switcher to combine these two pictures and, through a knockout effect, block out a portion of one camera's picture of the newscaster, which portion corresponds with the white letters in the other camera's picture. The combined picture is not a superimposition. It is a composite of two solid and opaque images, one within the other with no bleeding through.

The Matte

The *matte* is a variation of the key, except that instead of allowing the special effects generator to select the material with the highest luminance and inserting that into the picture with the lower luminance (as with our white-letters-over-newscaster example) the switcher makes the judgment about which picture is inserted into which. In the matte effect, the switcher can replace the white letters with gray or even black. Thus, a switcher can avoid, for example, placing white letters over a white portion of the background picture which would render the overall result somewhat illegible. Instead, the switcher can make the letters black or gray to produce greater contrast and thereby greater legibility. Some switchers come with a "joy stick," or wipe positioner, so the effects can be placed anywhere on the screen; some allow a black edge or border to be added to the picture inserted so it will stand out from its background picture.

The Chroma-Key

The *chroma-key* effect is the matte effect applied to color TV. Just as in the matte effect the special effects generator electronically removed any black or dark gray portion of the picture when combined with some

FIGURE 5-9a. Camera 1's Picture. (Courtesy of Cablevision Systems Development Co.)

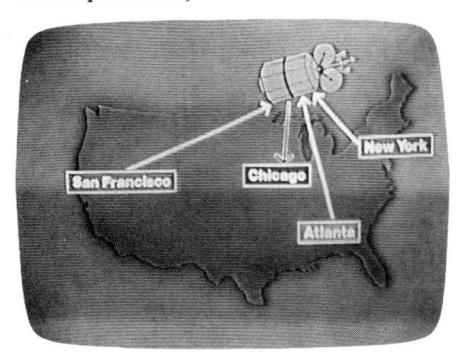

FIGURE 5-9b. Camera 2's Picture.

FIGURE 5-9c. Cam 1 Keyed into Cam 2. (Courtesy of Cablevision Systems Development Co.)

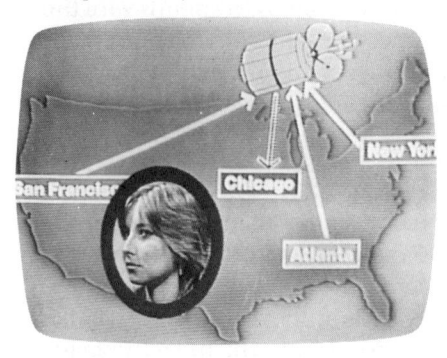

FIGURE 5-9d. Cam 2 Keyed into Cam 1. (Courtesy of Cablevision Systems Development Co.)

other background picture, in chroma-key the special effects generator can select any color of the TV spectrum (green, blue, red, or combinations of these primary colors) and remove it electronically and replace it with a picture from another camera. Blue is most often selected over red, for example, since blue is the color furthest from skin pigmentation. For example, a newscaster sitting before a background of evenly lit, saturated blue would be visible and opaque, providing he was not wearing any blue colored clothing and the background could be replaced with the picture on another camera.

The Wipe

One of the most practical of these "special" electronic special effects is the *wipe,* the electronic removal of one camera's picture and its re-

FIGURE 5-10. Vertical Wipe. (Courtesy of Cablevision Systems Development Co.)

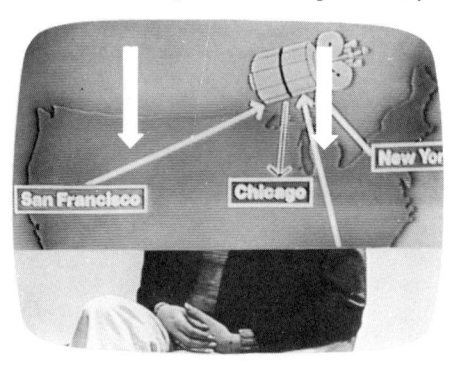

FIGURE 5-11. Horizontal Wipe. (Courtesy of Cablevision Systems Development Co.)

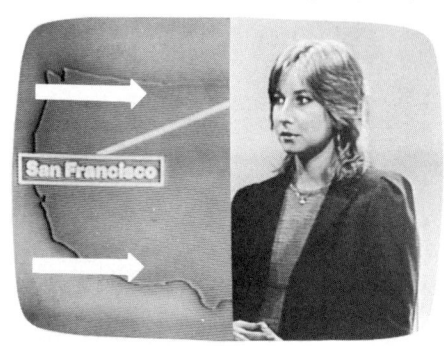

placement by another's picture. The most basic wipes are the *horizontal wipe* and the *vertical wipe*. Some confusion is caused by the terms horizontal and vertical in that they refer not to the axis of the line which separates both pictures but refer instead to the direction in which this line moves. Thus, a horizontal wipe means that one picture pushes the other from side-to-side, across the screen, not unlike closing or opening a shower curtain. A vertical wipe means that one picture pushes the other off the screen downward or upward, not unlike lowering or raising a window shade.

The Corner Insert

Again, the special effects generator adds an extra row of buttons and a second set of levers to the two-bus switcher. The buttons select the different patterns for corner inserts and the levers perform the wipe involved in executing the corner inserts. The buttons are marked with little diagrams indicating the pattern of the corner wipe and also indicate which portion of the composite picture will come from A bus and which will come from B bus. By placing the levers at the middle position the switcher causes the program monitor (or preview monitor if the mix button on the preview monitor is depressed) to show a composite picture analogous to the diagram on the button of the effect desired. One example of an especially suitable corner insert effect is when a person is giving a speech and a smaller picture of someone else is framed in one of the corners as he/she "signs" what is being said for the benefit of the deaf people in the TV audience. As the switcher moves one of the levers, the picture will widen or narrow the corner insert. Conversely, as the switcher moves the other lever, the inserted picture will shorten or lengthen vertically.

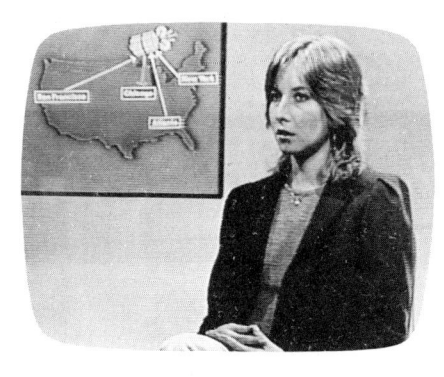

FIGURE 5-12. Corner Insert with black edge. (Courtesy of Cablevision Systems Development Co.)

Split Screen

With appropriate lever manipulation the switcher can lengthen the insert all the way and then use the other lever to move the split from right to left. This motion is called a horizontal wipe. Arresting this movement midway would provide an electronic special effect known as split screen. The most common use of split screen is to show both ends of a telephone conversation. A more creative, original use might be to show each of the fighters in a boxing ring between rounds as they get ready for the next round. Juxtaposing these two fighters on one split screen when in reality they are on opposite sides of a boxing ring would dramatize the confrontational situation that exists even between rounds.

6
THE TV DIRECTOR

This author's first experience in TV directing was in 1947 at the University of Wisconsin. The words that the instructor spoke as he pointed to the empty director's chair have not faded even with the passage of more than 35 years: "Go to it—just remember the TV director functions pretty close to the panic level—now relax!" However doubtful pedagogy that remark might have demonstrated, it did make the point that TV directing is a demanding, stressful activity.

The TV director must possess certain personality traits, some of them contradictory, and must demonstrate these various traits simultaneously. The TV director must perform many functions and perform them simultaneously. The TV director must have these traits and perform these functions simultaneously.

PERSONALITY TRAITS

1. The director must be friendly but firm as with any leader—friendly as possible, but firm as necessary.
2. The director must have a "take charge" attitude but also be sensitive to the problems and personality traits of those upon whom he/she must depend: talent, production crew, technicians. The director should not appear to be "using" them for a personal "ego trip."
3. The director should be poised but excited in a positive way about the program. Honest enthusiasm is better than a feigned blasé attitude.
4. The director should have a sensitivity regarding the "aesthetic" dimension of the program while recognizing and respecting the "technique" aspects of the production, the equipment, and the technicians.
5. The director must be—or at least appear—knowledgeable about the

craft and yet curious to know more and not too proud to ask for advice and help.
6. The director must have such managerial skills as orderliness and structured thinking and yet be alert and flexible enough to "think on his/her feet," to react to unanticipated problems and to take advantage of unforeseen opportunities that may develop.

FUNCTIONS OF THE DIRECTOR

What does the director do? Perhaps the answer to this question should be divided into what the director does in rehearsal, what the director does when the program is on the air, and what the director does after the program.

Prior to On-the-Air

The first thing a director must do is to become familiar with the program's script. There are three degrees of script completeness: the *fully scripted,* the *semi-scripted,* and the *rundown.*

The Script. A *fully scripted show* contains all the words that are to be spoken and the movements made by the talent in the program, usually typed on the right ⅔ of the page in a column labeled AUDIO. The left ⅓ of the page, in a column labeled VIDEO leaves room for the director to write-in camera angles, switching cues, lighting cues, and any other little notations to help him/her execute decisions during the actual on the air performance. These notations might include little sketches and drawings of stick-figures. The advantage of having a fully scripted show to direct is that it provides predictability and, therefore, control of what is about to happen. The director follows predetermined directions rather than having to make decisions on the run, as the program goes along, somewhat spontaneously. The main disadvantage is that except for shorter programs in which the director almost will have memorized the cues, a fully scripted show chains the director to the script thereby limiting his/or ability to devote attention to all the many other tasks to be attended to; further, a scripted show limits the director's ability to take advantage of a shot that did not occur to him/her during rehearsal, as well as limiting the flexibility to adapt to an unforeseen emergency that did not present itself during rehearsal. Dramatic shows, news programs, documentaries, political speeches, and commercials are types of programs which are fully scripted. A *semi-scripted* show is usually one in which spontaneity and adlibbing are expected and welcome, such as interviews, discussions, and quiz shows and other such free-wheeling exchanges. Usually such semi-scripted shows contain predetermined opening and closing remarks and some predetermined internal remarks to serve as cue lines for the director when transition points have been reached; in this way, the director will know when to roll film or have cameras move to another portion of the set. The semi-scripted show allows the director more freedom and allows for more spontaneity in pacing the show. The *rundown* script is an even more fragmentary blueprint for what is to transpire, leaving even more leeway and discretion for the director—but also more unpredictability. It is simply a check-list of activities to be engaged in with only very fragmentary indications of what is to be said. Directing with only a rundown is a somewhat chancy proposition perhaps best left to experienced persons on both sides of the camera.

Fully scripted and semi-scripted programs are the ones most frequently encountered in the small/medium-sized TV installation. Whatever kind of script is involved, the director is well-advised to begin thinking about and planning an approach as soon as the script is available and before arriving at the studio for rehearsal. As a director, one should make some tentative judgments regarding how the rehearsals and production will proceed, considering the format of the show, considering the type of subject matter, considering the personalities of the talent and their relationships to each other, considering the length of time for rehearsal time available and the length of the program, considering the size and nature of the studio and the set, considering the type and number of cameras and mikes available, and so forth. Having a tentative plan beforehand is much better than going into rehearsal cold and starting from ground zero.

Rehearsals. The director comes next to the decision regarding what style of rehearsal to conduct. There are three main types of camera rehearsal: *film style, stop-if-necessary,* and *continuous running* style. In the *film style,* the director dissects the script into smaller specific scenes, rehearses each segment until it is ready, and then tapes it. The individual snippets may not be taken in chronological order for rehearsal and taping, with the expectation—or at least the hope—that these pieces can be assembled into some cohesive order during the editing process later. Whatever perfection this procedure promises needs to be measured against the time, effort, and cost involved in this laborious process, usually regarded as too exotic for most programs encountered in small/medium installations. There is also the risk that when "spliced" together fluency and pacing may suffer and the aesthetic "seams" might show. The whole might be *less* than the sum of its parts. Related to the film style is what might be called the *stop-if-necessary* style in which the run-through proceeds until something goes wrong, at which time the rehearsal is stopped and is backtracked to a reasonable point just prior to the mishap and resumed at that point. The advantage of this method is that the sequence can be played back then and there on a studio or control room monitor and the director can show what he/she thinks went wrong and suggest changes to the members of the cast and crew. The *continuous running* style, perhaps a direct carry over from the pre-videotape recorder, "live" era during which there was no choice, is the traditional type of camera rehearsal, in which the run-through is continuous, except for the gravest mishaps, the minor mishaps being noted for correction later. Only with this method can the director, cast, and crew get to evaluate the pacing, rhythm, and momentum of the entire production while it is being presented. Frequently, especially in small/medium installations dealing with limitations of rehearsal time, budget, facilities and with relatively uncomplicated subject matter, the director does not have the luxury of choosing one of these luxurious rehearsal types. The decision may have been made by producers. The director may be allotted only 1½ times the actual running time of the program itself. In such situations, directors are well advised to spend most of their precious rehearsal time in the studio—rather than the control room—right on the front lines to show the talent and camera persons first-hand what they want them to do. Directors should stress the critical and complicated portions of the show—such as rising from a chair and walking across the set to an easel, or pointing a hand-held glossy photograph at the right angle toward the camera taking it so it does not glare, or rehearsing special effects, etc. The director, using a studio mike to give instructions to control room personnel—switcher and audio person—talks "live" to those in the studio with him/her—talent and crew. A control room program monitor and a studio monitor shows all concerned how at least the opening, the major transitions, and the closing should look. The main shortcoming of this abbreviated rehearsal schedule is the unpredictability—and therefore lack of control—that it imposes on the director and others, particularly in the area of clock time and psychological time. The director is forced to fly blind to a certain degree—and hope for the best.

When the director gets to the control room—having spent as much time as possible in the studio, he or she tries to recreate the picture he or she composed in the mind's eye before the rehearsal began, as well as those pictures that occurred to him/her in the studio during the walk-through camera rehearsal.

Script Marking. When the director enters the control room, he undertakes the marking of his script.

Although a number of script-marking symbols have come into general use, each director works out his or her own system of notation. After all, these symbols the director writes right into the script—in the video column and between the double or triple spaced lines—are reminders to himself/herself. These are some of the standard script-marking symbols:

SYMBOL	MEANING
F I	Fade-in
T	Take
D	Dissolve
SUP	Super
F O	Fade-out
Q	Cue
D I	Dolly-in
D O	Dolly-out
T R	Truck right
T L	Truck left
Ready 1	Get camera 1 ready
	Precise spot for switch
2 SH	Shot of 2 persons
3 SH	Shot of 3 persons
O/S	Over-the-shoulder shot
T C	Title card
C U	Close-up
E C U	Extreme close-up
M S	Medium shot
L S	Long shot
E L S	Extreme long shot

Again, the director comes to the studio with a reasonably specific idea of which cameras will take which shots—subject to change when the director tries out those shots. As each shot is achieved by the camera person to the satisfaction of the director, the camera person jots it down on the "shot sheet" and the director numbers each shot and enters it right into the script making an additional note of the camera number to which the shot has been assigned. Thus, the rehearsal period is devoted to arriving at a series of camera shots, audio and lighting effects, and talent activities; recording these activities by appropriate written symbols; and practicing them as much as time allows so as to have them readily available to the director before he or she needs to call for them during the actual program broadcast or taping. The opening pages of a dramatic script written and directed by this author some years ago that use some of the standard script-markings for a fully scripted program are shown on pp. 126–128.

On-the-Air

The function of a TV director while the program is on the air is not unlike that of a symphony conductor. The conductor's role and function essentially involve a process of coordination. The musicians have been rehearsed sufficiently so that the conductor is satisfied enough with the level of performance to present the production to an audience. The conductor is not a one-man-band. In fact, the conductor does not play any instrument in the performance, but he or she has coached and motivated (perhaps inspired) the members of the group not only to do their utmost but to coordinate their contribution with that of the others so that they play as an ensemble—as opposed to a bunch of individual musicians each going his/her own way. An orchestra is more than the sum of its parts. Similarly, the element that galvanizes the separate components of TV production into a cohesive, aesthetically satisfying whole is the director. He or she is the glue that holds the mosaic together.

To be sure, not every TV program is expected—or intended—to be a work of art, especially the modest rehearsals usually encountered in a small/medium installation. Nevertheless, even in the case of the simplest lecture/demonstration involving one performer, the director's job is a challenging one. Specifically, what things does the director do—and do simultaneously—during the actual show?

1. The director must give instructions "live" to those members of the crew with him/her in the control room and over the intercom to those members of the crew in the studio. The director must listen to and respond to questions or suggestions coming from any member of the crew in the studio or the control room.
2. The director must watch the program monitor critically so he/she will know what the audience is seeing (or the audience watching the videotape later will see) to be sure that what he/she intended to show is really there.
3. The director must watch the monitor showing the picture he/he wants to show next to be sure it is ready to be shown and, if not, order those changes that will make it ready. In an unscripted show, the director must

BLIND--AS A BAT
by Frank Iezzi

VIDEO   AUDIO

Scene I
FI Film, music + sound
(ESTABLISHING FILM SEQUENCE   MUSIC: LONELY, BROODING
SHOWING LIGHTHOUSE WITH SEARCH-   SOUND: OMINOUS SOUND OF
LIGHT SWEEPING SKY) **sup C1 Graphic**   CHURNING SEA, SOUND
                                             UNDER ENTIRE SCENE
GRAPHIC: BLIND--AS A BAT

Lose C1, Fade music
(DAN AND TIM IN BOBBING ROWBOAT
ABOUT TO DISEMBARK ONTO SMALL
DOCK AT FOOT OF LIGHTHOUSE)

D C2, 2SH + Q _____   TIM: (Lifts canvas sack of pro-   1
                                           visions onto dock and climbs
                                           up after it)

                                           How much time will I have
                                           Dan?

                                     DAN: These are treacherous waters 2
                                          even when there ain't a blow
                                          a' brewin'!

T C3 CU _____   TIM: How much time?   3

T C1 MS _____   DAN: (Secure heavy hemp rope   4
                                          to mooring post)

                                          I've got to make it back
                                          past these reefs and back to
✻ Q (LIGHTNING FLASH) _____   the ship before she weighs
                                          anchor without us. I figger
                                          that gives you thirty min-
        ✻ Q _____   utes, lad!
                                          (THUNDER CLAP ONE SECOND
                                          AFTER LIGHTNING FLASH)

T C2 2 SH _____   TIM: Thirty minutes to tell the   5
                                          old captain we have come to
                                          take him away because he's
                                          not fit to do even this God-
                                          forsaken job!

                                     DAN: Havin' to keep an eye on the 6
                                          old captain won't make rowin'
                                          no easier for me!

T C3 CU _____   TIM: The old captain! Funny we   7
                                          should still call him that!
                                          I was with him when they
                                          told him he was too old to
                                          sail as a skipper. Something
                                          seemed to snap inside him,
                                          Dan.

126

T(C2)2SH   DAN: That's when you got him this   8
                     job as lighthouse keeper?

                TIM: The sea's all he's ever   9
                     known, Dan. He'd die if he
                     could be near it! (Looks
                     toward the top of the light-
                     house) And now I've got to
                     be the one who takes it all
                     away from him!

                DAN: You've done your best, lad.   10
                     Makin' this trip through
                     these treacherous waters to
                     bring him supplies every
                     month--and comin' alone to
                     keep anyone from knowin' he
                     was going blind! How bad was
                     it last time?

T(C3)CU   TIM: The captain's completely   11
                     blind now, Dan!

T(C1)MS   DAN: What'll he do when you tell   12
                     him it was you who told the
                     authorities he was goin'
                     blind? And that you're to
                     take his job as lighthouse
                     keeper? Let me come up with
                     you!

T(C2)2SH   TIM: To protect me from a blind   13
                     old man?

T(C1)CU   DAN: Be careful, lad. (Takes from   14
                     his pocket an old-fashioned
                     pocket watch) Remember, I
                     leave at midnight! It's now
                     11:30!

T(C3)2SH   TIM: (Starts to open heavy door,   15
                     pauses) You know Dan--if it
                     was just his blindness I
                     wouldn't have told the au-
                     thorities--.

                DAN: What else is there, lad?   16

T(C2)ECU   TIM: I'm afraid the captain is
                     losing his mind!

127

Cut sea sound + Q   MUSIC: / STINGER CUE

Scene II
(CUT TO INTERIOR OF LIGHTHOUSE
SHOWING CONCAVE WALLS)

T③ WS   CAPTAIN: / (Suddenly stops pacing,   18
stands taut and poised like
a pointer who had detected
some sound)

T① MS
Is that you, Tim? (When he
senses Tim is about to enter
ZOOM TO CU   th room) Why are you so late? /
(Fingers the hands of a clock
whose glass has been removed)
It's after 11:30!

T② WS   TIM: / (Arrives at the top of spiral   19
stairs, enters out of breath)
There's a blow comin' up!
It was hard getting through
those shoals!

T① MS   CAPTAIN: / Never mind! Sit down, Tim,   20
and listen to me carefully--

T② MS   TIM: / Captain, there's something   21
I've got to tell you--

T③ 2SH   CAPTAIN: / (Impatiently) Sit down, Tim.   22
I've got something to tell
you--but promise you won't
say anything until I've
finished telling you--

         TIM: But captain, I--(Sits down   23
resignedly)

T① CU   CAPTAIN: / Remember a year ago when my   24
eyes first started to fail
me and I made you promise
to keep my secret? You have
kept it, Tim--you're the
only one I can trust--

watch all the monitors not on the air to see which offers him/her the best shot.
4. The director must watch the script to know when to instruct the switcher to change to the next picture. A director who becomes too engrossed in the markings on the script to watch the monitors would be like a driver watching the road map instead of the road.
5. The director must time the program. Timing involves not only *mechanical*, real, clock time but *psychological* time as well. *Mechanical time* is measured by the control room wall clock and the stop watch. The show as a whole and any inserted segments must not run too long or too short. *Psychological time* refers to how long or how short the program *seems*. Is it dragging or lacking in momentum and, if so, how can the director "punch up" the proceedings? Conversely, is the lecture/demonstration moving too quickly to be absorbed by the viewer and, if so, at what point and how can the brakes be put on?
6. The director must be aware of the sound of the program, even though there are more than enough drains on his/her attention in connection with the *looks* of the program. Is the opening theme music drowning out the opening announcement? Is the performer falling off mike into inaudibility as he/she walks across the set to the easel? Is the audio on the film insert synchronized with the picture? Is the audio quality "right" for what is being seen on the program line?

To bring order out of this potential chaos, a special vocabulary has been developed. It is a special shorthand designed to expedite the giving of instructions to the crew by the director and to standardize somewhat the jargon used by various TV installations. To simplify the listing of these terms they are divided into separate categories—*camera cues, switching cues, audio cues*—and then combined in a typical sequence in which they might be combined immediately before the beginning and immediately after the beginning of a hypothetical program.

SPOKEN CUE	MEANING
Camera Cues	
"Pan right!"	Camera person rotates camera horizontally toward the camera person's right causing the image to move left in the viewfinder and control room monitor.
"Pan left!"	Camera person rotates camera horizontally toward the camera person's left causing the image to move right in the viewfinder and control room monitor.
"Tilt up!"	Camera person makes the front of the camera point upward causing the image to move downward in the viewfinder and control room monitor.

Camera Cues

"Tilt down!"	Camera person makes the front of the camera point downward causing the image to move upward in the viewfinder and control room monitor.
"Pedestal up!"	Raise the camera head to a higher level above the studio floor.
"Pedestal down!"	Lower the camera head.
"Dolly in!"	Move entire camera directly toward the set.
"Dolly out!"	Pull the camera directly back away from the set.
"Truck right!"	Camera person moves entire camera toward the right parallel to the set.
"Truck left!"	Camera person moves entire camera toward the left parallel to the set.
"Single shot!"	Camera person frames one person.
"Two shot!"	Camera person frames two persons.
"Three shot!"	Camera person frames three persons.
"Group shot!"	Camera person frames entire group.
"Over-the-shoulder shot!"	Camera person frames back of shoulder of one person in foreground while showing front of another person in background.
"Cover shot!"	Camera person gets wide enough shot to show the entire scene.
"Frame up!"	Camera person uses discretion in centering and balancing components of a picture.
"Focus up!"	Camera person makes sure lens is giving the sharpest focus for the shot.
"Zoom in!"	Camera person adjusts the zoom lens so that the image is brought closer to the camera while still keeping the proper framing and focus.
"Zoom out!"	Camera person adjusts the zoom lens so that the image is moved further from the camera while still keeping the proper framing and focus.
"Loosen shot!"	Camera person dollies-out or zooms out to move image away from camera.
"Tighten shot!"	Camera person dollies-in or zooms in to bring image closer to camera.

Audio Cues

"Let's get a level!"	Performer provides a sample of voice level so audio person can adjust microphone volume.
"Ready to open mike—Open mike!"	Audio person throws switch to make microphone operate.
"Standby with music!"	Audio person readies record or tape of music.
"Bring in music!"	Audio person releases record or starts tape and gradually raises volume.
"Hit music!"	Audio person brings in music abruptly at full volume.
"Music up!"	Audio person increases volume.
"Fade music!"	Audio person lowers volume until it disappears.
"Music down and under!"	Audio person lowers volume but does not remove it entirely.

Switching Cues

"Ready to fade-in cam 1!"	Switcher depresses button #1 on unused bus opposite lever and places forefinger on lever.
"Fade in one!"	Switcher moves lever to bus on which button #1 is depressed.
"Ready to take cam 2!"	Switcher places forefinger on button #2 on live bus.
"Take 2!"	Switcher depresses button #2.
"Ready to dissolve to cam 3!"	Switcher depresses button #3 on idle bus and places forefinger on lever.
"Dissolve to 3!"	Switcher moves lever to idle bus which has depressed button #3.
"Ready to lose cam 1!"	Switcher depresses button #1 on idle bus and places forefinger on lever.
"Super 1!"	Switcher moves lever to midpoint between busses.
"Ready to lose cam 1!"	Switcher places forefinger on lever ready to move it away from the bus on which button #1 is depressed.
"Lose 1!"	Switcher moves lever to bus that is opposite to the bus with the depressed button #1.
"Ready to fade to black!"	Switcher depresses button on idle bus to which no video source is connected—a blank button.

Switching Cues

"Fade to black!"   Switcher moves lever to bus with newly depressed button attached to no video source.

Again, the job of the TV director is to coordinate the efforts of the camera person, the audio person, the switcher, and the talent. The following is a sequence of cues a director might give for the opening of a hypothetical TV program being videotaped. All the director's cues and orders are heard live by the crew members in the control room with the director and are heard over the intercom system by the crew in the studio. The talent in the studio can hear any remarks the director makes over the studio loudspeaker before airtime but the director is precluded from using the studio loudspeaker during the program because the sound would be picked up by the mikes on the set and thereby be recorded on the videotape. Any messages the director would like to send to the talent during the program taping must be relayed to them through the floor person and communicated by sign language or by cue cards.

CUES PRIOR TO AIRTIME	ACTIONS TAKEN
"Three minutes to air; audio person check levels, please!"	Audio person double checks volume of talent's mikes and of record or audiotaped music (or sound).
"Two minutes to air; floor person can you hear me? Camera 1? Camera 2?"	Director announces 2 minute warning into intercom and/or over studio loudspeaker; floor person repeats warning aloud in studio; director double checks intercom and headset connections.
"One minute to air; opening shots; ready to roll VTR tape!"	Director specifies *VTR* tape as opposed to audiotape; floor person repeats aloud one minute warning cue.
"Thirty seconds; roll VTR. (To floor person) Standby—ready to cue announcer. (To switcher) Ready to fade-in camera #1 (To audio person) Ready to open announcer's mike and ready to bring in music."	Floor person shouts "Standby!" to alert announcer; switcher depresses button #1 on bus opposite lever; audio person cues up record or audiotape and gets ready to flip switch opening the announcer's mike.

CUES AT AIRTIME

"Fade-in 1!"   Switcher moves lever to bus with button #1 depressed.

"Hit music!"   Audio person engages turntable record or rolls audiotape and simultaneously opens pot for that sound source.

"Music down and under!"	Audio person turns down (but not completely out) the music.
"Ready to open announcer's mike; ready to cue announcer; open mike and cue announcer!"	Audio person flips switch to open announcer's mike; floor person cues announcer to start speaking.
"Ready to dissolve to camera 2; ready to open interviewer's mike; ready to cut interviewer to camera 2; ready to fade out music—dissolve to 2, open interviewer's mike, fade out music, cue interviewer to 2!"	Switcher depresses button #2 on idle bus and on command "Dissolve" moves lever to depressed button #2; audio person turns down volume on record or audiotape and flips switch to open interviewer's mike; floor person cues interviewer to camera 2.

POSTPRODUCTION: THE VIDEOTAPE RECORDER

Few technical developments have had as profound an effect on TV production in general, and the director's role in particular, as the videotape recorder (VTR). Quite simply, in the pre-VTR days all TV production was "live production." Even though TV shows could be "recorded" by making a film of a monitor showing the TV program as it was taking place (the process known as *kinescoping*), the program had to proceed nonstop, without interruption—"live." The poor reproduction not withstanding, the miracle of directing live TV—like the singing dogs on the Johnny Carson show—was not how well it was done but that it was done at all! This writer has not yet fully recovered from having to direct live hour-long dramas in the pre-VTR days; such an experience makes today's TV director's trauma pale by comparison. Considering the fact that the average "life span" of an individual camera shot is about 12 seconds before it is replaced by the picture on another camera, a 60-minute program meant about 300 individual shots! The feeling was something akin to terror, especially since the TV director has to spend most of the time during the actual program watching the monitors and not blindly reading cues from the script. Like the driver trying to find his way through a new town, whose attention needs to be on the road, not on the road map, the director of a live show needed to focus on the program, not the script. This meant *almost* memorizing the 300 shots! The VTR changed all that—though the memory lingers. Now the TV director, except for time and budget constraints, can keep on doing a scene until everyone gets it right! In fact, the director can call in the cast and crew after a particular segment has been taped, *show* them what he/she wants changed, and have them try it again. The tyranny of the clock has been lessened somewhat along with some of the director's tension.

Not only has the advent of the VTR reduced the nerve-wracking aspects of the director's job, but it is virtually an essential item of equipment in the nonbroadcast TV situation, in which most small/medium TV installations find themselves. Without the VTR not only would TV programs have run a specified length and have to be presented at a specified time of day, but without the VTR there would be no trace, no record (except for the unsatisfactory "kinescope") of its having been presented. The convenience videotapes provide of being able to prepare a program at a convenient time, before it is to be "consumed," has had an impact on the TV industry at least as considerable as frozen foods have had on the food industry—with the even more astounding fact that the videotape—unlike the frozen TV dinner—can be consumed repeatedly rather than just once! Preparing a TV program live for showing just *once* was a highly wasteful procedure, particularly for small, closed-circuit TV audiences. Kinescopes were unsatisfactory not only because of poor technical quality, not only because cost of film stock and film processing made it expensive, but also because kinescopes (essentially a film picture of a TV picture) took some time to process. You did not know what you had until it came back from the processing lab—and then it was too late to do anything about it. At the risk of becoming too anecdotal—an occupational hazard of us pioneer old-timers in TV—this writer has a bitter memory of such a disaster involving kinescopes. One time many years ago at the University of Wisconsin, we devoted an entire semester to doing an hour-long adaptation of *Medea*, with full costume and make-up and with a first-rate cast; when it was kinescoped, we blithely sent it off to be processed, proud of our efforts and accomplishment. Weeks later, we reassembled to see the processed kinescope and perhaps bask in the glory of our accomplishment—only to find out that the audio had not been recorded on the film! The entire hour-long film was *silent,* making it of interest only to lip readers. The audio person who neglected to throw the audio switch left the party early. The rented costumes had been returned, the sets had been disassembled, the studio equipment had gone on to other uses, the cast had scattered—there was no chance to do it again. A VTR would have avoided the disaster.

The VTR usually is located in the control room in the small/medium TV situation and usually is operated by the switcher (technical director). This brief treatment of the VTR might have been included in the section dealing with the switcher but since the VTR is so closely related to postproduction editing (which is usually done by the director), this consideration of the VTR and its uses is included here in the section on the TV director.

The first VTR that came upon the scene in the late 1950s was the quadruplex videotape recorder, so called because it employed four separate "heads." The Quad VTR recorded almost vertically on 2-inch videotape. The quad machine is still recognized as the only full professional VTR by professional broadcasters, but its initial cost, the cost of engineering time to maintain it, the sheer bulk of the machine and storage space for the 2-inch videotape reels, make it less than ideal for the small/medium TV installation. Next came the helical scan, slant-track VTR, so called because it records diagonally on a slant (almost horizontally) across the tape rather than in a transverse (almost vertical) manner of the quad VTR. Although the helical scan is less stable and reliable than the quad VTR video signal, the helical scan video signal can be enhanced to become as reliable as the quad VTR video signal, and helical scan videotapes can be dubbed onto 2-inch quad tapes. Helical scan formats (widths) offer a wide variety of options. Most common is the 1-inch tape, but ½-inch and even ¼-inch tapes are available. Videocassettes (videotapes sealed or semi-sealed in plastic boxes) for helical scan VTRs use ¾-inch tape and some sophisticated helical scan VTRs even use 2-inch videotape.

There are basically two types of helical scan VTRs likely to be encountered in the small/medium TV installation: *reel-to-reel* and *cassette/cartridge*.

FIGURE 6-1. Reel-to-Reel Videotape Recorder. (Courtesy of Sony Corporation of America.)

FIGURE 6-2. Videocassette being erased (bulked). (Photograph by Francis De Petris.)

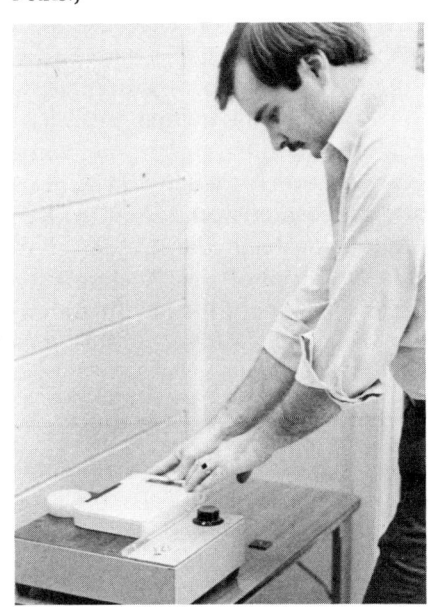

The reel-to-reel VTR involves threading the tape from the supply reel to the take-up reel in much the same manner as threading an audiotape recorder. There is usually a threading diagram handy, imprinted on the VTR or on the inside cover. Care should be exercised to avoid smudges, fingerprints, or crinkling of the tape. The threading should be done with the machine *off* so there is no slack in the tape. Cassette/cartridge tapes come in a plastic box and involve no threading. There is a difference between a cassette and a cartridge. The cassette comes in a plastic container that can be opened and which contains a supply reel and a take-up reel that can be rewound. The cartridge is permanently sealed in a plastic box and contains a single reel. When it is inserted into the VTR slot it becomes threaded automatically in much the same way as an audio cartridge.

VTR Controls

Some of the controls on the VTR are similar to those on an audiotape recorder. *Play* advances the tape from the supply to the take-up reel, past the recorder heads during playback and record. *Record* engages the recording heads for the audio and the video as the tape advances while the *play* button is depressed. *Play* and *record* must be depressed simultaneously, in order to avoid accidental erasing of the tape. *Fast forward* advances the tape rapidly. *Rewind* moves the tape back from the take-up reel to the supply reel at a rapid rate. *Stop* brings the motion of the tape to an abrupt halt. Some VTRs have a *standby* button which permits the heads to come up to full rotating speed before the tape is advanced. Some VTRs come with a *variable speed* control that allows the tape to move faster or slower, forward or reverse. Some VTRs have a *freeze frame* control that permits the tape to be stopped briefly to examine an individual frame. Some VTRs are equipped with *automatic gain* controls for video and audio levels while some VTRs have video and audio meters that have to be monitored by someone during the taping—probably the switcher in the small/medium setup. Just as with the VU monitor described in the section on the audio console, an occasional kick of the needle into the red portion would be permissible but the proper range should be used most of the time.

Videotape Editing Methods

One of the most primitive ways of editing videotape is the *cut-and-splice* method, almost identical to the process used for editing audiotape. The sequences to be joined are cut diagonally in a splicing block, the ends are butted together, mylar-based splicing tape is placed across the joint, and the excess splicing tape on either side is trimmed. Physically editing videotape is to be avoided except when absolutely necessary. Physical editing of videotape is not satisfactory because it does not take into account the sync control track signal recorded along the length of the videotape. The signals on each of the sequences are not likely to be synchronized and the result is a distracting picture roll at the point of the splice. Another shortcoming of the cut-and-splice method is the risk that some of the adhesive between joints will seep through and gum-up the audio and video heads. In addition, cutting expensive videotape whenever a splice is needed is a wasteful and expensive practice, especially in the small/medium TV situation.

To overcome these considerable shortcomings of physical-mechanical editing, a new method was developed: *electronic editing* which involves no actual cutting of the tape. Instead, the video signal on one stretch of videotape is transferred to another videotape. It is really a process of re-recording rather than of cutting. One method of electronic editing—less primitive than physical cutting of the tape but still unsatisfactory—is by making VTR-to-VTR edits. Two VTRs are involved: one to serve as *playback* (or master) VTR and the other to serve as *recording* (or slave) VTR. Both VTRs have monitors to "monitor" what each VTR is doing. Simply place a blank tape on the recording (or slave) VTR, which we can label VTR 2. Then load the playback (or master) VTR, which we can label VTR 1, with the original video sequence you want to transfer. The signal goes by cable directly from VTR 1 into VTR 2. Simply start VTR 2 rolling, push the recording button and then push the start button on VTR 1. When the portion of tape you want from VTR 1 has finished, stop, rewind and remove the tape and reload VTR 1 with the next tape you want to add to the new composite tape. This process of adding on additional segments to make one composite tape is known as *assembly editing* and it is the type used for most of the editing done in video. A second type of editing is called *insert editing*. As the name implies, this involves replacing one segment of a recorded videotape with another segment of equal length without having to record the adjacent sequences. Although better than physical editing, the results of VTR-to-VTR editing are less than perfect. One can expect at least some momentary break-up of picture and sound at the electronic "seams" between tape sequences when the composite tape is played back.

The small/medium TV installation is likely to do its videotape editing either by using a VTR that is equipped with an editing capability or else with a separate machine known as an *editing control* system. A VTR with editing capability is known as an *editing deck*. It does everything an ordinary VTR does but it has extra electronic components

FIGURE 6-3. ¾" Videocassette Editor. (Courtesy of Panasonic Corp.)

FIGURE 6-4a. Editing Control System. (Courtesy of Panasonic Corp.)

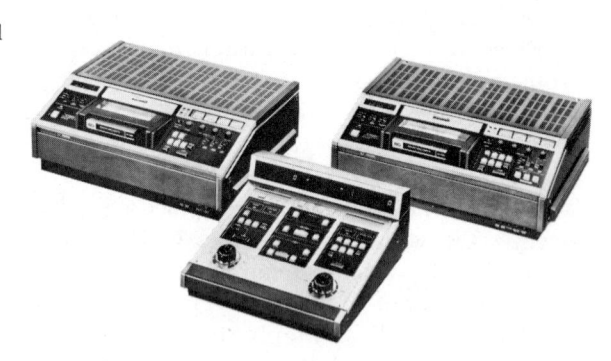

FIGURE 6-4b. Portable Editing System. (Photograph by Francis De Petris.)

FIGURE 6-4c. Editing Control Box. (Courtesy of Panasonic Corp.)

which make electronic editing possible. If an editing deck is used in place of VTR 2 mentioned in the VTR-to-VTR example mentioned above, the potential incompatibility in sync when the signal changes at transition points where separate tapes are joined is lessened. Thus, the picture "roll" or "break-up" or "glitch" is usually avoided. Much better than using an editing deck is the use of an editing control system, consisting of two cassette editing decks connected by a control box. This box makes the entire process of finding edit points automatic and even offers remote control operation, slow motion search, digital tape counter, and even preview capability. As with many other items of TV equipment, the more small/medium TV installations seek to acquire editing control systems, the lower the price becomes and the more small/medium TV installations can afford them. By whatever editing equipment the budget allows, the TV director in the postproduction process made possible by the invention of the VTR, splices together the individual segments of tape to turn out a cohesive, creative, accurately timed end product, without having to do it "live" at the time it is being consumed, with all the extra tension that process involved.

GLOSSARY

Aspect Ratio. The relationship between the height and the width of the TV screen, the ratio being 3:4 units of measurement.

Assemble editing. A procedure for electronic editing of videotape whereby one sequence is attached to previous sequences to build up an entire program.

Audio Level. The strength of an audio signal, usually measured by the activity of the needle on a volume unit.

Audio mixer. A console that blends various sounds from different sources into one composite sound which represents the proper mixing of the individual sounds, usually accomplished by turning rotary knobs or raising or lowering slide-faders.

Audio Track. The portion of the videotape that is used to record the sound portion of a program.

Background Light. General lighting of the backdrop, or cyc, to lend perspective to those elements on the set.

Back Light. Light from directly behind the subject to set it off from the background and to lend a three-dimensional effect.

Barn Doors. Metal flaps on the sides, top, and bottom of a light to mask off a certain portion of the light thrown by the lighting unit.

Base Light. The general, overall lighting which lights the entire set in order for the camera to obtain a satisfactory picture.

Bi-directional. The pick-up pattern of a microphone that accepts sounds from two opposite directions.

Blast Filter. A sponge rubber attachment that covers a microphone to reduce the popping sound made by explosive sounds.

Boom. A metal structure that supports a microphone, a light, or a camera to bring any of these three as close as possible to the subject without being seen in the TV picture.

Broad. A floodlight with a flat reflector that provides diffuse, soft, general light.

Bulk Eraser. A mechanism that creates a strong magnetic field to erase the magnetic patterns on an audiotape or a videotape.

Burn-In. The retention of an image on a camera tube after the camera has moved to another subject, frequently the result of having left the camera pointing too long at the same subject—particularly if the subject is brightly lit and contains extreme contrast.

Bus. A row of buttons on a switcher.

Bust Shot. Framing of a camera shot of a person from the chest upward.

Cameo Lighting. A lighting effect in which the subject in the foreground is brightly lit and the background is black.

Camera Chain. Used to denote the TV camera itself, the camera control unit, the power supply, and the sync generator.

Camera Control Unit. Controls used by the video technician before and during the program to regulate brightness, contrast, and balance.

Camera Light. A small spotlight affized to the top of the camera so it moves as the camera moves to provide fill light directly on the subject.

Cam Head. A mounting for the camera head that enables the camera to pan and to tilt smoothly.

Cardioid. The heart-shaped pick-up pattern of a microphone.

Cartridge. A plastic box containing an audiotape or videotape for recording or playing back which rewinds and recues itself.

Cassette. Similar to a cartridge except that it contains a supply reel and a take-up reel that can be opened; some cassettes can rewind themselves automatically.

Character Generator. An electronic mechanism that operates with a key to produce numbers, letters, and other graphic information on a television screen "live" during a program or stored on a floppy disc before needed in the production.

Chroma Key. An electronic special effect that enables image from one camera to be inserted into the image of another video source; a "key color," usually blue, is removed from the one picture and is replaced by the background image of another video source.

Close-up. Camera shot in which the subject is seen up front, filling the entire frame.

Color Temperature. A meter measurement of the reddish and blueish characteristics of light measured in degrees of Kelvin.

Condenser Microphone. A sensitive, wide frequency response microphone with a vibrating plate and a fixed back plate for modulation.

Contrast Ratio. The ratio between the darkest portion and the lightest portion of a picture.

Control Room. That area of the TV center in which the director, audio person, and switcher sit to control the audio and video aspects of the program and sometimes the lighting aspects of the show; sometimes the control room contains a double-glass window which looks into the studio.

Control Track. That portion of the videotape that contains information employed and synchronize the playback and editing operation in videotape production.

Corner Insert. A special effect consisting of curtailing the vertical and horizontal scan of one camera's picture and inserting the curtailed scan of another camera's picture into the empty space provided in one of the quadrants of the screen.

Cradle Head. A camera head mount that connects the camera head to the pedestal or tripod and allows smooth movement of the camera head—particularly tilting movement.

Crane. An oversized boom structure on which a TV camera and a camera person are mounted to permit very high and very low angle shots; can move very smoothly while on the air.

Crawl. A studio device for providing moving lines of print up or across a TV screen to provide credits.

Credits. Names and job titles of major persons involved in the TV program, usually shown on the screen near the end of the program by means of a moving crawl or individual graphic cards or by means of a character generator.

Cross Fade. The simultaneous fade out of an audio source, a camera picture, or a lighting effect as another is faded in.

Cucalorus. A metal pattern that is inserted into an ellipsoidal light to cast a shadow pattern.

Cue. A signal to begin an activity, usually preceded by a warning that such a signal is imminent.

Cue Card. A large card the floor person holds next to the lens of the camera so the talent can refer to it for lines or cues; a prompting device.

Cut. A switching command to replace one picture on the line monitor with another picture instantaneously.

Cyclorama. A U-shaped, continuous piece of fabric that covers the back wall of a TV studio.

Decibel. A measurement unit applied to the relative intensity or power of a particular sound as compared to other sounds.

Depth of Field. The distance in which the nearest and the furthest objects in a picture can remain in focus using a particular lens without moving the camera; depends on distance between camera and subject as well as on f-stop and focal length of the lens in question.

Dimmer. Mechanism for regulating the amount of electrical power reaching a lighting instrument thereby affecting the amount of light output of that instrument.

Director. The member of the production team who has ultimate responsibility for how a TV program ultimately looks and sounds.

Dissolve. The gradual removal of one picture by the switcher and its gradual replacement by another picture.

Diversity Receiving System. A feature some wireless microphones possess for eliminating interference and signal drop-out.

Dolly. To move the entire camera toward or away from the set; the structure on wheels or casters that enables the camera to be moved smoothly in the studio.

Dual Redundancy. A precautionary measure whereby twin mikes are provided so that if one mike breaks down the other picks up the sound automatically and without interruption.

Dubbing. Duplicating the recorded material on an audio—or video—tape to provide extra copies that are one generation away from the original.

Dynamic Microphone. A sturdy yet sensitive microphone that operates by a diaphragm attached to a moveable coil.

Easel. A structure used in the studio to support graphic cards.

Echo. The repetition of a sound after that sound has ceased to be made, sometimes an unwanted phenomenon but sometimes consciously done for effect.

Editing Deck. A videotape recorder equipped with circuitry for insert and assembly editing of video information contained on another videotape recorder.

Effects Bus. A row of buttons on the switcher used to achieve such special electronic effects as wipes, inserts, keys, etc.

Electret Condenser Microphone. A compact microphone that contains its own battery source of power built right into the microphone.

Electron Beam. The stream of electrons sent by the electron gun.

Electron Gun. The mechanism found at the back of the camera tube and the receiving tube, used to fire the electron beam.

Electronic Editing. Assembling individual segments of video material into a composite according to a predetermined order by re-recording material from such individual segments.

Electronic Viewfinder. A small TV monitor usually located on top of the camera to enable the camera person to see what the camera is "taking."

Ellipsoidal Spotlight. A spotlight which gives hard, directional light, equipped with metal shutters to control light distribution and a slot for inserting a cucalorus pattern.

Erase Head. An electromagnet that erases an audio or videotape before new information is recorded on it.

Essential Area. The center area of a graphic card that contains all of the visual information the viewer will see even after any cropping that might occur in transmission due to misalignment of the home receiver.

Establishing Shot. An overall shot of the scene before tighter shots are taken, in order to orient the viewer, usually shown near the beginning of the program.

Fade. The gradual introduction of a picture out of black or the gradual removal of a picture to black, analogous to fading-in or fading-out of a sound source.

Fader Lever. In video, a lever on the switcher used to create fades, dissolves, supers, wipes, and split screens; in audio, a pot or slide fader used to increase or decrease volume of sound.

Fill Light. Usually provided by floodlights to fill in dark shadows created by key light and to lend a three-dimensional effect and to reduce the contrast ratio.

Film Chain. Sometimes known as telecine, contains a multiplexer, one or two film projectors, a slide projector, and a stationary TV camera to translate optical pictures into electronic pictures for television.

Fishpole. A hand-held boom to which a microphone is attached, used mostly on remote broadcasts.

Fixed Focal Length Lens. A lens that has one focal length as contrasted with a zoom lens that has variable focal length.

Flag. A rectangular metal sheet that prevents light spill or is used to cut off part of a light beam.

Floor person. Person responsible for the studio crew and for relaying to the talent the instructions of the director who is in the control room during a program.

Focal Length. The distance between the optical center of a lens to the point at which the image is in focus.

Focus. The point at which the image "taken" by a lens is at its clearest and best defined.

Frame. One complete, individual television picture consisting of two interlaced fields and lasting 1/30th of a second.

Frequency. The number of vibrations per second of a sound wave.

Frequency Response. The range of frequencies that a microphone is able to pick up.

Fresnel. A spotlight featuring a lightweight lens employing a series of concentric ring steps to cast a beam of hard light.

f-Stop. The numerical setting on the barrel of a lens which indicates the aperture; the larger the number the smaller the aperture and vice-versa.

Fully Scripted. Refers to a program for which all dialogue is written out as it is to be spoken leaving no opportunity for adlibbing or spontaneity.

Gain. Refers to the amount of signal amplification, with regard to video and audio signals; "riding gain" refers to keeping the level of various sound sources at the proper levels.

Giraffe Boom. Microphone support that is smaller than a perambulator crane but larger than a fishpole boom, used to get the microphone close to the person speaking but not in the television picture.

Glitch. A momentary interruption in the scanning of a picture.

Graphics. Refers to two-dimensional visuals whether they be camera cards, crawls, slides or electronic symbols produced by a character generator.

Gray Scale. Variations in shades in a TV picture ranging from TV black to TV white with eight shades of gray in between.

Hand Cue. A visual, silent cue given by the floor person to the talent during a program.

Hard Light. Light coming from spotlights characterized by dark shadows and high contrast ratio; primarily directional strong light.

Head Room. The space left just above the subject's head and below the top of the frame.

Headset. A mechanism consisting of two earphones and a mouthpiece which connect the wearer to the intercom system connecting the control room and the studio so conversations can be conducted without the audience hearing what is being said.

Helical Scan. Otherwise known as "slant track," a videotaping process by which the video information is put on the tape in a long, diagonal slanted way as opposed to transverse scanning which is almost horizontal.

High Z. A high impedance microphone signal.

Hue. The basic color of a TV color picture, as opposed to saturation and luminance.

Image Orthicon. Camera tube mostly in use during the 1950s and 1960s, since largely replaced because of their bulkiness by smaller, more compact tubes, such as the vidicon tube.

Image Retention. A "burn-in," sometimes temporary, sometimes permanent, on the camera tube, caused by the taking of a static, brightly lit, high contrast picture too long; when temporary, it is also known as "lag," "smear," or "comet tailing."

Joystick. A control found on most special effects generator switchers to position a cut-out pattern anywhere on the screen.

Key. An electronic special effect whereby an opaque image on one camera is inserted into the background picture of another camera.

Key Light. The principle source of illumination falling on a subject or a scene causing deep shadows.

Keystone. Distortion caused by photographing a flat graphic from an angle too different from perpendicular.

Kicker. A supplementary light usually placed to the side and rear of the subject to lend more of a three-dimensional impression.

Kinescope. A film made of a TV program while it is on the TV screen, the only recording method before the advent of videotape.

Lavalier. A miniature microphone worn on the clothing of the performer or fastened by a cord around the neck.

Lead Room. Analogous to head room except that it involves space on the sides of a figure, either walking or stationary.

Lens. Optical glass disc with curved surfaces for focusing light on a surface, as with camera lens as it focuses light image on the face of the camera tube.

Lens Turret. A flat plate in front of nonzoom cameras which contains several lenses of different lengths each of which can be positioned in front of the camera tube by rotating the plate by a hand-grip at the back of the camera.

148 *Glossary*

Light Grid. A series of pipes at right angles to each other hung just below the ceiling of a TV studio, from which lighting instruments are hung.

Light Meter. Instrument for measuring the intensity of incident and reflected light on a subject.

Light Ratio. The relative intensity of the light sources, including key, fill, back, side, and kicker lights.

Line Monitor. The monitor that shows the final picture chosen by the director to be taped or to be sent to the home viewer.

Long Shot. A view of a scene seemingly from a great distance using a wide angle of view, used for "establishing shots."

Low-Z. Low impedance microphone signal in wider use than high-Z because it allows the use of longer cables.

Luminance. The "brightness" channel in a color camera which is used to provide the proper contrast for the color signal and to be sure proper contrast is maintained for monochrome receivers still in wide use, the latter consideration a matter of federal law.

Matte. An electronic special effect by means of which one image on a camera can be cut into the background image of another camera with the use of a special effects generator.

Mechanical Editing. Editing of videotape by actually cutting and splicing the tape, not desirable except in extreme emergency; generally replaced by electronic editing.

Medium Shot. A camera shot somewhere between a long shot (which shows a lot of background) and close-up shot (which shows almost no background behind the subject).

Mix Bus. Two rows of buttons on a switcher connected by fader levers to produce cuts, fades, dissolves, and supers.

Mix/Effects Bus. Additional rows of buttons and levers and joysticks on a special effects generator to produce inserts, keys, wipes, and split-screen effects.

Multiplexer. A system utilizing mirrors and prisms that sends pictures from film projectors and slide projectors into a stationary TV camera to convert optical images into electronic images.

Normaled. A wiring circuit permanently installed between studio and audio console, a direct link that can be changed through the use of patch cords in the patch panel.

Normal Lens. That lens with a focal length that comes closest to making the scene appear as it would appear to the eye of a viewer from that distance.

Objective Time. Real, actual time as measured by a stopwatch or studio clock, as opposed to subjective time.

Omni-Directional. Sometimes known as nondirectional, refers to the pick-up pattern of a microphone that picks up sound from all directions equally well.

Over-the-Shoulder Shot. Camera includes in the shot the shoulder and back of the head of one person while it takes a more open view of another person.

Pattern Projector. A metal cut-out inserted into an ellipsoidal spotlight to cast shadow patterns on a background or cyclorama.

Patch Board. A panel of sockets by means of which video, audio, and lighting instruments are connected to their controls.

Patch Cord. The double plugged cord to effect connections on the patch board.

Pedestal. The base upon which the camera mount and camera head are placed; also, the command to raise the level of the camera head.

Polar Pattern. A schematic representation of the pattern of pick-up of a microphone, usually represented two-dimensionally but actually a three-dimensional phenomenon.

Pot. Short for potentiometer, the control for regulating the volume of sound from a sound source.

Preview Bus. Row of buttons that allows the director to check out a camera shot or a special effect before he has it put on the air or on the videotape.

Preview Monitor. The monitor in the control room on which the picture being previewed is shown.

Prism Beam Splitter. A prism block that replaces the complicated mirrors and prisms and filters in earlier color cameras to separate the three primary colors in the color TV picture.

Program Bus. The row of buttons on the switcher whose inputs go directly to the line monitor when they are punched up.

Quadruplex. A videotape recording process using four separate heads and using 2-inch videotape, as contrasted with the helical scan process.

Rear Screen. Translucent screen used in the studio against the back of which an image is projected from a slide projector and photographed by the TV camera from the front.

Reel-to-Reel. An audiotape or videotape recorder that moves the tape from a supply reel, past the recording heads, to the take-up reel and requires hand-threading, as opposed to cassettes or cartridges.

Ribbon Microphone. Delicate microphone that functions as a ribbon vibrates within a magnetic field; sometimes known as a "velocity" mike.

Rundown. The least detailed version of a script, in which the sequence of activities is listed but not the actual dialogue to be spoken.

Saturation. The aspect of a color that indicates its strength and purity, undiluted by white.

Scanning. The movement of the electron beam across and down the camera tube to change light energy into electrical impulses and, at the receiving end, across and down the home TV set.

Scanning Area. The picture that is taken in by the camera and shown on the control room monitors and the camera viewfinder, subject to cropping after transmission.

Scoop. A floodlight, providing diffuse, scattered light usually to serve as fill light.

Scrim. A spun-glass filter placed in front of a light to diffuse and soften the lighting effect.

Segue. An audio effect whereby one sound source is removed and immediately replaced by a second sound source without interruption.

Shotgun Mike. A microphone which is highly directional, used when subjects are at some great distance from the holder of the microphone, as in sporting events, etc.

Shot Sheet. A list of individual shots given to the camera person by the director, which shots he/she should make available for the director to use.

Sidelight. A supplementary source of light which illuminates the side of a person to make the picture more three-dimensional.

Slip Cue. A procedure for cueing up a record by the audio person so the sound will be available without delay when called for by the director.

Softlight. An unfocused lighting instrument which floods the scene with general, diffused illumination.

Special Effects Generator. A device on some switchers to permit exotic electronic special effects, like wipes, keys, mattes, etc.

Splice. A physical cutting and joining of videotape or audiotape.

Split Screen. A horizontal wipe that is interrupted half-way through so the previous image and the new images share the screen equally.

Spotlight. A lighting instrument that gives a directional, highly focused beam of light.

Stop Down. To reduce the size of the aperture of a lens to let less light through.

Stretch. A hand and arm silent signal from the floor person to the talent to take more time with what he/she is doing.

Striplight. A group of broads attached to each other, usually to light a broad area like a cyclorama.

Subjective Angle. Positioning and locating the camera so the scene is shown from the participant's point of view.

Subjective Timing. As opposed to actual, clock time, how long a program or segment *feels* rather than *is*, sometimes known as psychological time.

Super. Short for superimposure, which involves an intentional double-exposure in which two pictures are shown simultaneously, usually printed material over a background picture.

Supercardioid Pick-up. A microphone whose pattern of pick-up is extremely directional, such as a shotgun microphone.

Switcher. A console (and its operator) containing rows of buttons and levers to make possible the change from one video source to another when, and as, ordered by the director.

Sync Generator. A section of the camera chain which produces synchronizing pulses for the camera tube and the TV receiver tube.

Take. A director's command synonymous with "Cut," which means to push the button for the desired video source so it will appear on the line monitor immediately.

Tally Light. Lights in the camera viewfinder, on the front of the camera, and on the control room monitors which glow when that particular camera's picture is being taken.

Telecine. The film chain where optical images are converted into electronic images.

Teleprompter. A device for mechanically moving a projected image of printed material over a glass screen in front of the lens so talent can read or refer to it while seeming to look right into the lens.

Three-Point Lighting. A generally accepted photographic principle which suggests that a key light provide the main light, that a fill light fill in some of the shadows to reduce contrast ratio and that a back light be used to separate the subject from the background and to provide three-dimensionality.

Trim. To adjust the barn-doors or shutters of a lighting instrument or to place "flags" in front of a light beam to confine it further and prevent light spill.

Truck. A director's command to the camera person to move the entire camera to the left or right, parallel with the set.

Tungsten-Halogen Lamp. Lamp used in quartz lights, featuring a filament encased in a gas-filled tube.

Unidirectional. The pick-up pattern of a microphone that picks up sound from only one direction.

Video. The picture portion of the television program.

Videocartridge. Permanently sealed, one-reel plastic box containing short videotape for recording and playback, rewinds itself after use.

Videocassette. Plastic box containing a supply reel and a take-up reel of videotape used for recording and playback of programs on a videotape recorder.

Video Monitor. A studio or control room TV set that shows the picture in high quality detail before it is transmitted to the home receiver. Unlike the home TV receiver, it does not have channel selector or volume control capability.

Videotape Recorder. A device for recording and storing the video and audio portions of a TV program for later use.

Vidicon. A camera tube that is smaller, cheaper, and sturdier than the image orthicon tube it has largely replaced.

Viewfinder. A miniature TV receiver usually atop the camera that enables the camera person to see what his camera is "taking."

Volume Meter. A meter on the audio console that measures intensity of volume of a sound source.

Wide Angle Lens. A lens with a short focal length that offers a wide viewing angle.

Wireless Mike. A microphone with a built-in FM transmitter which eliminates the need for microphone cables and makes concealment and moving about much easier for the talent.

Zoom Lens. A variable focus lens that can bring the viewer close-up to the talent or way back from it—or any point in between—without having to physically move the camera.

BIBLIOGRAPHY

BRETZ RUDY. *Techniques of Television Production,* 2nd edition. McGraw-Hill Book Company, New York, 1962.

BURROWS, THOMAS D., and WOOD, DONALD N. *Television Production: Disciplines and Techniques.* Wm. C. Brown Company, Iowa, 1980.

CHESTER, GIRAUD, GARNET R. GARRISON, and EDGAR E. WILLIS. *Television and Radio,* 5th edition. Prentice-Hall, Inc., New Jersey, 1978.

MILLERSON, GERALD. *The Technique of Television Production,* 10th edition. Focal/Hastings House, New York, 1979.

MILLERSON, GERALD. *TV Camera Operation.* Hastings House Publishers, New York, 1973.

MILLERSON, GERALD. *TV Lighting Methods.* Hastings House Publishers, New York, 1975.

ROBINSON, RICHARD. *The Video Primer.* Quick Fox Books, New York, 1978.

STASHEFF, EDWARD, RUDY BRETZ, JOHN GARTLEY and LYNN GARTLEY. *The Television Program: Its Direction and Production.* Hill and Wang, New York, 1976.

UTZ, PETER. *Video User's Handbook.* Prentice-Hall, Inc., New Jersey, 1980.

WILLIAMS, RICHARD L. *Television Production: A Vocational Approach,* 2nd edition. Vision Publishing, Utah, 1981.

WURTZEL, ALAN. *Television Production.* McGraw-Hill Book Company, New York, 1979.

ZETTL, HERBERT. *Television Production Handbook,* 3rd edition. Wadsworth Publishing Company, 1976.

INDEX

Aesthetic considerations of lighting, 36–38
Aspect ratio, 61–62
Assembly editing, 137
Audio, 2–32
   control room activities, 23–32
   cues, 129, 131
   studio activities, 2–22
Audio cartridge recorders, 23, 31–32
Audio consoles, 23–26
Audio plugs, 20–21
Audiotape recorders, 23, 28–31
Audio turntables, 23, 26–28

Background-light, 45, 47–48
Back-light, 45–48
Balanced lines, 20
Barn-doors, 40, 43, 50
Baselight, 34–35
Base of camera, 88–91
Beam knob, 102–3
Bidirectional microphones, 3, 6–7
Boom microphones, 8–9
Brightness, 101

Brightness control knob, 102
Broad lights, 40, 43
Bus (*see* Switching)
Bust-shot (BS), 77

Cables and connections, microphones and, 19–20
Cam head, 92
Camera, 74–104
   base, 88–91
   cues, 129–30
   head, 93–104
   mounting head, 91–93
   pictorial compositions, 82–88
   shots, 74–82
Camera angle, 74, 78–82
Camera-light, 49
Carter-Ford presidential debate, 18
Cassette/cartridge videotape recorders, 135–36
Character generator, 66, 67
Chroma-key, 114, 115–16
Chrominance channels, 100
Close-up (CU), 76

155

Color temperature, 36
Condenser microphones, 3
Continuous running style rehearsals, 122, 123
Contrast control knob, 102
Contrast ratio, 36, 37, 49
Corner insert, 117
Cradle head, 92
Crawls, 67, 70
Cropping, 62–63
Cross-fade, 28, 111–12
Cucalorous patterns, 40, 41, 42
Cue cards, 57–58
Cueing up, 27–28
Cues:
 at airtime, 132–33
 audio, 129, 131
 camera, 129–30
 hand, 54–57
 prior to airtime, 132
 switching, 129, 131–32
Cut-and-splice editing, 30–31, 136–37
Cuts, 108–9
Cyclorama strip lights, 43, 44

Dead (bleed) area, 62
Dead center framing, 83, 85
Depth of field, 52, 95
Desk microphones, 8
Diffusers, 49–50
Dimmer board, 50–51
Director, 120–39
 floor person and, 54–61
 on-the-air functions, 125, 129–33
 personality traits, 120–21
 rehearsals, 122–23
 script and, 121–22
 script marking, 124–28
 videotape recorder and, 133–39
Dissolve, 109, 110
Dolly, 88, 93, 97
Donahue show, 18
Drag controls, 93
Dynamic (pressure) microphone, 2–3

Easels, 67–68
Editing:
 cut and splice method, 30–31, 136–37
 videotape methods, 136–39
Editing control system, 137–39

Electronic editing, 137–39
Electronic principles of camera tube operation, 99–100
Ellipsoidal spotlights, 39, 40
External sync, 103
Extreme close-up (ECU), 76–77
Extreme long shot (ELS), 74, 75

Fade, 28, 109–10
Field of view, 74–77
Fill-light, 45–48
Film style rehearsals, 122–23
Filter/equalizers, 27
Fishpole boom, 8, 9
Fixed focal length single lens, 94
Flaps, 50
Floodlight banks, 40
Floodlights, 39, 40
Floor lights, 44–45
Floor manager (*see* Floor person)
Floor person, 54–71
 as contact with talent, 61
 as director's surrogate, 54–61
 as studio troubleshooter, 60
 (*see also* Graphics)
Floorstand microphones, 8
Fluorescent banks, 40, 42
Fluorescent lamps, 38–39
Focal length of lens, 94, 95
Focus, 94
Four-bus switcher, 112–13
Four-shot, 78
Framing, 82–83
Fresnel spotlights, 39–40, 49
Front projection, 67, 71
f-stop, 94, 95
Full-shot (FS), 77
Fully scripted show, 121–22

Gain, 24, 26
Giraffe boom, 8, 9
Glare, 68–69
Graphics, 61–71
 displaying and handling, 67–71
 principles in design, 61–65
 production, 65–67
Gray scale, 64
Group shot, 78

Hand-held microphones, 10, 11, 18
Hand signals, 54–57
Hanging microphones, 8

Hard light, 37
Head room, 82, 84–85
Head-shot (HS), 77
Helical scan videotape recorder, 135
High angle shot, 80
High impedance, 19–20
Highly directional (super-cardioid) microphones, 3, 5–6
Horizontal hold knob, 102
Horizontal wipe, 116, 117
Hue, 64–65, 100

Illusion of depth, 82, 85–87
Image orthicon (IO) tube, 98
Impedance, 19–20
Incident light, 35, 36
Insert editing, 137
Internal sync, 103

Key, 114–15
Key-light, 45–48
Keystoning, 68
Kicker-light, 48–49
Kinescope, 133, 134
Knee-shot (KS), 77
Kroy technique, 65–66

Lavalier microphones, 10, 11, 18
Lead space, 85, 86
Lenses, camera, 52, 94–98
Lens turret, 94, 96
Lettering, 65–67
Lighting, 34–52
    aesthetic considerations, 36–38
    control, 49–52
    instrument placement, 45–49
    in studio (*see* Studio lights)
    technical aspects of, 34–36
Light meter, 35–36
Live production, 133, 134
Long (narrow angle) lens, 94
Long shot (LS), 74, 75
Low angle shot, 79, 80
Low impedance, 19–20
Luminance channels, 100–101

Matte, 114, 115
Mechanical focus knob, 103
Medium shot (MS), 74–75

Microphones:
    cables and connections, 19–20
    mounting and placement, 7–18
    pick-up patterns of, 3–7
    plugs, 20–22
    selection, 2–6
Monaural sound, 30
Mounting head (camera), 91–93
Moveable microphones, 7, 8–10

Nondirectional microphones (*see* **Omnidirectional microphones**)
Normal angle shot, 78–80
Normal lens, 94
Nose room, 84–85
Number of persons shown, 74, 78

Omnidirectional microphones, 3–4
One-shot, 78
Overhead angle shot, 81–82
Overhead pipe grid, 43, 45
Over-run lamps, 38
Over-the-shoulder angle shot, 81, 82

Panning, 88, 92–93
Panning handle, 92, 93
Patch-bay, 50–51
Perambulator boom, 8–9
Persistence of vision, 99
Personal microphones, 7, 10, 18
Pick-up patterns of microphones, 3–7
Pinned beam, 40
Plugs, microphone, 20–21
Plumbicon tube, 100
Pneumatic pedestals, 89, 90
Polarity, reversing, 37
Polar pattern, 3
Portion of subject shown, 74, 77–78
Postproduction, 133–39
Potentiometers (pot), 24, 26, 29
Pre-amplifiers, 24
Preview bus, 112, 113
Program bus, 112–13
Psychological closure, 83

Quadruplex videotape recorder, 135
Quartz lamps, 38

Reality switching, 106, 108–9
Rear projection, 67, 71
Reel-to-reel videotape recorders, 135–36

Reflective light, 35, 36
Rehearsals, 122–23
Reverse angle shot, 81, 82
Ribbon microphones, 3
Riding gain, 24, 26
Rule of thirds, 83
Rundown script, 121, 122

Safe title area, 62
Saturation, 64–65
Scanned area, 62
Scoop lights, 40, 42, 44
Script, 121–22
  marking, 124–28
Segue, 28
Semi-scripted show, 121–22
Setting the tracking, 97–98, 103
Short (wide angle) lens, 94, 95
Shot box, 97
Shotgun microphones, 8, 10
Shot sheet, 124
Sidelight, 48
Slide-faders, 24–25
Slides, 67, 69
Snoots, 50
Softlight, 37, 40, 43
Special effects, 106, 109–12
  electronic, 113–18
Splicing process, 30–31
Split screen, 114, 118
Spotlights, 39–40
Spread beam, 40
Stage manager (*see* Floor person)
Stationary microphones, 7, 8
Stereo sound, 30
Sticking, 102–3
Stop-if-necessary style rehearsals, 122, 123
Strip lights, 40, 42–43, 44
Studio-field pedestals, 88–89
Studio lights, 38–45
  bulbs, 38–39
  housings, 39–43
  supports, 43–45
Studio pedestals, 89–91
Subjective angle shot, 80–81
Super, 109, 110–12, 114
Supplementary area, 62

Switching, 106–18
  cues, 129, 131–32
  electronic special effects, 113–18
  reality, 106, 108–9
  special effects, 106, 109–12
Switching board, 106, 107
Symbols, script-marking, 124, 126–28

Talk space, 84–85
Tally lights, 103
Target knob, 102
Technical aspects of lighting, 34–36
Technical directors, 106
Telecine island, 69–70
Teleprompters, 58–59
Television director (*see* Director)
Three point lighting, 45–47
Three-shot, 78
Tilting, 88, 92, 93
Time cards, 57, 58
Time cues, 57
Tripods, 88
Truck, 93
Tube, camera, 98–101
Tungsten (incandescent) lamps, 38
Two-shot, 78

Unbalanced lines, 20
Unidirectional (cardioid)
  microphones, 3, 4–5

Velocity (ribbon) microphones, 3
Vertical hold knob, 102
Vertical wipe, 116, 117
Videotape recorder (VTR), 133–39
Vidicon tube, 98–100
Viewfinder, camera, 101–4
Volume unit (VU) meters (volume indicators (VI)), 25, 26, 29

Waist-shot (WS), 77
Wipe, 114, 116–17
Wireless (FM) microphones, 10, 11, 18, 19

Zoom lens, 94, 96–98
Zoom range, 96